GOVERNING CHINA

150–1850

Governing China

150–1850

John W. Dardess

Hackett Publishing Company, Inc.
Indianapolis/Cambridge

Copyright © 2010 by Hackett Publishing Company, Inc.

All rights reserved
Printed in the United States of America

14 13 12 11 10   1 2 3 4 5 6 7

For further information, please address
Hackett Publishing Company, Inc.
P.O. Box 44937
Indianapolis, Indiana 46244-0937

www.hackettpublishing.com

Cover design by Abigail Coyle
Text design by Mary Vasquez
Maps by William Nelson
Composition by Cohographics
Printed at Sheridan Books, Inc.

Library of Congress Cataloging-in-Publication Data
Dardess, John W., 1937–
  Governing China : 150–1850 / John W. Dardess.
    p. cm.
  Includes bibliographical references and index.
  ISBN 978-1-60384-311-9 (pbk.) — ISBN 978-1-60384-312-6 (cloth)
  1. China—Politics and government. 2. China—Social conditions.
3. China—History—Han dynasty, 202 B.C.–220 A.D. 4. China—History—
Qing dynasty, 1644–1912. 5. Political culture—China—History. 6. Social
institutions—China—History. 7. Education—China—History. I. Title.

DS740.2.D37 2010
951—dc22   2010015241

The paper used in this publication meets the minimum requirements
of American National Standard for Information Sciences—
Permanence of paper for Printed Library Materials, ANSI z39.48–1984.

Contents

Preface	vii
Introduction: Comparing China in 150 and China in 1850	x
Timelines	xxiii
Maps	xxvii

PART 1. FROM FRAGMENTATION TO REUNIFICATION, 150–589	1
The Unraveling of the Later Han, 150–220	3
The Three Kingdoms, 221–264	5
The Western Jin, 266–311	6
A Fractured Age, 311–450	8
Unity in the North: The Northern Wei, 398–534	12
Not by Blood Alone: Steps to Reunification, 534–589	16
PART 2. IMPERIAL GRANDEUR AND ITS AFTERMATH, 589–907	19
Unification by the Short-lived Sui, 581–618	22
The Long-lived Tang, 618–907	23
The Tang as Empire	26
After Empire: Reconstructing China	28
Confucianism and Buddhism in the Late Tang	30
The Shattering of the Tang, 868–907	32
The Five Dynasties and Ten Kingdoms, 907–960	34
PART 3. THE TRIPARTITION OF CHINA, 960–1279	36
The Liao (927–1125), Northern Song (960–1126), and Xi Xia (982–1227)	38
The Jin (1115–1234), Xi Xia (982–1227), and Southern Song (1127–1279)	45
New Developments in the Southern Song	47
The End of Tripartition	49
PART 4. PERMANENT UNITY LARGELY ACHIEVED: YUAN, MING, AND QING, 1271 TO 1850	52
Yuan China, 1271–1368	61
The Creation of Ming China, from 1368	66

The Ming Refounded: Jianwen (r. 1398–1402) and Yongle (r. 1402–1424)	69
The Middle Years of the Ming	71
The Reign of Jiajing, 1522–1566	73
Late Ming Foreign Relations	76
The Late Ming: Internal Developments	78
The Ming Collapse, from 1627	80
Qing China: The Founding, from 1644	82
The Conquest of South China, 1644–1683	84
Beyond China: Building the Qing Empire	86
Refocusing on China: Yongzheng, r. 1722–1735	88
The Reign of Qianlong, 1735–1799	89
Social Institutions in Political Context	91
Further Reading	103
Index	107

Preface

My excuse for writing this short book is just a guess—that it might prove useful for students of China and the occasional general reader to have at hand a concise and accessible account of what happened among, and to, that huge agglomeration of people we call Chinese at the east edge of the Eurasian landmass over a very long segment of their recorded history. Originally, it was the Italian editors of a multiauthored set of books about China who invited me to contribute a long section on that topic within the 150–1850 time frame. The idea made immediate sense to me, and I accepted the invitation. The present offering revises and expands a bit on what I wrote for an Italian readership.

Why focus on governing, and why adopt this particular time frame? I take governance to be both the ultimate barometer as well as the ultimate determinant of the well-being of human society and its panoply of activities. The institutions of government and the men and women who assume the governing positions reach us individually only occasionally, but they always affect us generally. This is because governments must try above all else to enforce order and ensure physical security to all within their borders. Political history is the ongoing story of how these things are done, or not done, over such and such a landscape over a given stretch of time. This basic matter is crude and easily stated, but the detail is infinite in its variety and complexity. The long story line ever fascinates with its triumphs and disasters, its marches to victory, its collapses in ignominy, its what-ifs, its who-is-to-blames, its factional struggles, its great stars, its cruel and corrupt villains, its good administrators, its feeble dupes, and on and on.

I found myself enjoying the writing of this little book. I liked reading up on a very large body of recent scholarship on Chinese history. I also found meaningful resonances with my own sense of autobiographical place in the larger story of the governance of the United States in the mid-to-late twentieth century: the mobilization of family members into the war against the Third Reich; the Cold

War that followed; Georgetown University; the U.S. Army's demand for Chinese-language specialists; the Army Language School; the Army Security Agency and its listening post on Taiwan; Columbia University; the University of Kansas—all large and powerful institutions set in a larger context of national needs and security, whose various missions gave definite form and direction to my own life's course. I have witnessed from afar three different Chinas in my lifetime: first, the miserable, war-torn, and starving China as shown in current events films to us grade school children in the late 1940s; then, the frightening Red China with its human-sea tactics, nuclear bombs, Great Leap Forward, and such horrors; and now, since the late 1970s, the gradual emergence of an authoritarian and repressive China as a great economic power and sober global actor. Both governance in general, and China's governance in particular, intertwine with my own biography.

As for the time frame, the years 150 to 1850, the choice appears practical to me. It would be physically nearly impossible to try to cover *all* of China's past in one short book. Besides, both early China and modern China enjoy strong and compact communities of interested scholars, students, and readers. The intervening 1,700 years are by contrast so divided among specialists in the various dynasties and topical fields that the whole span seems to consist—misleadingly—of completely discrete and unrelated bits. Tang experts seldom have much to say to Ming specialists; religious historians rarely venture into military affairs. So there is an opportunity here to address the whole long story and tease out the main lines of coherence and development. And the years 150 and 1850 serve fairly well as bookends in a narrower sense. In 150, the long-lived Han realm, for centuries the dominant power in East Asia, reached a point of deflection and downspin into civil war, ruin, and, seventy years later, collapse. By 1850 the Qing, also the dominant East Asian power, reached a similar point and it too collapsed—sixty years later. Foreign monks and the originally Indian religion of Buddhism rose to places of prominence in China after the Han fall; Marxism, Comintern personnel, and Western ideas and advisers of all sorts entered China soon after the fall of the Qing. In both cases, China's educated people sought answers to terrible domestic problems. The falls of the Han and Qing produced two very different developments, then, that in some ways trace similar trajectories. What else comes up if one compares the years 150 and 1850? It is intriguing to note that in 150 China was not far from the eve of great apocalyptic uprisings, including especially the Yellow Turban outbreak of 184. In 1850, Qing China was also about to explode in rebellions, among which the largest was the millenarian Taiping rebellion of 1850–1864. Both rebellions came to base themselves in the more thickly settled parts of the China of their time; significantly, both shared the goal of *taiping* ("great peace" or "great leveling"); and while both were eventually suppressed, the suppression was made possible only by an eventually fatal devolution of power downward from the imperial center to the regions and provinces. Between 150 and 1850 only one rebellion rivaled those outbreaks in scale and ferocity, and that was the Red Turban affair of 1351–1354, also millenarian, which engulfed all of China and led, indirectly, to the collapse of the Mongol Yuan dynasty. Many other popular risings, to which central governments were extremely sensitive, erupted during times in between. But broader comparisons than this between the late Han and the late Qing can be drawn as well and to those this book now turns.

Introduction

Comparing China in 150 and China in 1850

Modern scholarship seldom addresses itself to the question of comparing China at two such remote moments in time as 150 and 1850, so one is forced to wade a bit into unexplored territory to perform such a comparison. That said, one cannot but be impressed by the durability of China's political, social, and educational institutions over the 1,700 years from 150 to 1850, from the time of Antoninus Pius, say, to that of Queen Victoria. Durability, but not rigidity. If one were to compare the institutions of the Later Han dynasty of 150 to those of the Qing of 1850, the similarities are of gross features, not of detail. These similarities can be explained in part by the persistence of environmental constraints (which were very different for Antoninus Pius and the queen), plus the continuity of the written language and the perennial emphasis in China's educational curriculum on the study of history and the Confucian classics. The compilation and preservation, dynasty after dynasty, of institutional monographs, encyclopedias, and other written guides made it no difficult matter to discover in great detail how governments of the past had been structured.

As for the environment, it may be said that China long occupied the best land in all of Eurasia. Once upon a time, thousands of years ago, East Asia could boast one of the richest and most varied endowments of plants and animals to be found anywhere on earth. Unlike species-poor Europe and North America, China was never defaced by glaciers. First to be thickly settled, farmed, and made to sustain a civilized polity was north China, with its rich soils, from roughly the second millennium BCE. A long and slow process of immigration from the north added south China to this core. By about 1000 CE, the south's population rose to parity with that of the north. In 1000 CE, China—most of it under the rule of the Northern Song dynasty—was beyond question the largest and wealthiest organized society in the world.

But what nature generously endowed with one hand, it flogged with another. China proper was, and still is, susceptible to prolonged and devastating droughts, and to catastrophic floods in the several great river systems that flow west to east across its territory. From very early on, it became incumbent upon the rulers of this rich land to defend the realm against encroachment from without and also to devise means to alleviate the effects of drought and flood within. By 150 CE, when our story begins, China had already developed a sophisticated and organized bureaucracy at the central and local levels, had assembled a copious repertory of ideas and techniques for governing the people, and had long and detailed written records available showing how these ideas and techniques had worked, or failed to work, in the past.

By 150 CE, the main principles of China's general strategy had been laid; and when our story ends, in 1850 CE, for all the changes that had occurred over those 1,700 years, the principles are recognizably the same. What were they? First, that the main business of China was China. Empire building, that is, the occupation of Inner Asian and other territory not inhabited by Chinese people, or Chinese speakers, was an occasional policy grounded mainly in security concerns. Empire was costly and simply never paid economic dividends. China was rich; territory beyond China was, comparatively speaking, poor. The pursuit of global commercial dominance by sea, as with the famous Ming flotillas of the fifteenth century, was also inordinately expensive. The Ming ventures were cancelled after a quarter century of operations and were never resuscitated. So China might pursue empire, but it might also withdraw—as it did in the Later Han (25–220 CE), the Tang (after 755), and the Ming (1368–1644)—without major damage. Thus the focus of China was, preeminently, China.

This leads directly to the second principle: that the purpose of any Chinese government was to protect the people of China from the vagaries of nature, from external enemies, and from themselves; to provide peace and tranquility and good order, so that happy and productive lives might be enjoyed by all, and the future made secure for everyone's children and grandchildren. Policies, and the institutions necessary to their realization, were designed accordingly. Often they worked well. Sometimes they worked badly, or not at all. There were intense disagreements over basic policy, as there was often more than one way to achieve a desired end, with momentous institutional consequences attendant upon the choice, as in the eleventh-century Northern Song.

There is a third set of principles observable in the story of China from 150 to 1850. Whether controlling all of China, or only a fragment of it, the government was always a monarchy. In addition to a military component, such monarchies always featured an ordered and ranked bureaucracy. These bureaucracies could range from small and docile groups of advisers and functionaries in the service of a warlord to large (20–50,000) meritocracies recruited through the national Confucian civil service examination system, minutely regulated, riddled with factions—some self-absorbed, some corrupt—yet often with a strong sense of rectitude and even moral superiority that monarchs often came to fear and resent. It might be argued that the most fundamental constant of all was the Confucian extended family system, which proved capable of adapting to and surviving almost anything: flood, drought, "barbarian" invasion and rule, murderous internal banditry and warfare, migration, opulence, poverty, agrarianism, commercialism, anarchy, new religions, and much else. Closely connected with the strength and durability of the family system was education—the desire of families and extended families to transmit literary skills and the knowledge of classical Confucian texts to their junior members (predominantly but not exclusively the boys). From this educated pool came the bureaucrats who helped rulers govern China. (I should like to defer a further discussion of family institutions to a later point in this book.)

Looking back from 1850 to 150, two simple facts disturb the image of a unitary "China" ruled by ethnic "Chinese." For 60 percent of those 1,700 years, China was ruled in whole or in part by an avowedly non-Chinese ruling dynasty. For 40 percent of that time, regional dynastic states shared rule over Chinese-inhabited territory. Only for 40 percent of the time did a "Chinese" ruling house rule all of a unitary "China" (the end of the Later Han, the Jin, the Sui, the Tang, and the Ming). So if there were a typical year between 150 and 1850, it featured either a non-Chinese ruler, a divided political landscape, or both. But toward the end of the span, that is, from 1279 to 1912, "China" was more typically united.

The institutional profile of China as compared at those two moments, 1,700 years apart, suggests that there was always something slippery in the interface between government and people. No amount of fine tuning in the internal ordering of government in the interim managed fully to surmount this problem.

Confucian theory laid down that legitimate government enjoyed a mandate from Heaven, a mandate that was contingent upon the ruler's ability to instruct the people and to protect and preserve them from human and natural harm; Heaven would punish serious failures in these respects by licensing the people to overthrow ruler and government and replace them with a new regime with a new mandate. Although the leaders of the great rebellions of 184, 1351, and 1850 espoused apocalyptic doctrines of Daoist, Buddhist, or Christian origin, respectively, they still gathered their forces within the standard Confucian paradigm of celestially mandated dynastic change and hoped to found dynasties. Whereas such giant outbursts were rare, smaller ones were not uncommon, and the leaders of many of them also found it expedient to announce an intention to found new dynasties.

What of the interface between government and society? Over the very long term, there were gross similarities and some subtle but important differences in the ways in which the Han and the Qing met the people. In the Later Han, and in every subsequent dynasty down to and including the Qing (founded in 1644), the lowest unit in the control of the central government was the *xian* (commonly translated as "county")—of which there were 1,179 in 140 CE, serving a population of some fifty million, and some 1,360 in 1850, ruling a population in the 300–400,000,000 range. Qing magistrates thus had five times the burden of their Later Han counterparts. County magistrates were the bottom tier of central appointees in both the Han and Qing. In the Han, the magistrate controlled some hundreds of subordinate officials and clerks, organized into around a half dozen specialized bureaus for litigation, markets, and the like; below the counties lay approximately 3–6,000 districts, and under them 12–29,000 communes, each with officials in charge of policing, tax collection, and other such tasks. All these officials and functionaries appear to have been salaried. In 1850, we find, once again, some hundreds of subordinate officials and clerks, an even larger number of messengers and runners, and roughly a dozen specialized county bureaus. Yet despite the greatly increased workload, the size of the county magistrate's staff and subordinates changed hardly at all. What this implied for the nature of China's ruling systems will be noted in due course.

Nor were those all the changes in governing from the Han to the Qing. In 150, the Han magistrate could reach downward via salaried functionaries into the subcounty units of district and commune. In 1850 the Qing magistrate had no such reach, insofar as unsalaried local conscripts staffed the subcounty units. Thus Han local government would appear to have been much the denser and the more closely controlled, with tax requirements that were commensurately heavy. Qing government was, by comparison, very cheap. The breakdown of the Later Han and the inception of four centuries of disunion are strongly linked to antagonisms of long standing between local government and locally powerful landed magnates controlling armed serfs. The central government feared and distrusted these people, yet it was they who provided the means to quell the Yellow Turban rebels, and it was they who a few years later helped bring about the Han downfall. In 1850, by contrast, locally powerful lineages never openly challenged Qing hegemony as they mobilized soldiers and successfully rallied to the dynasty's defense against the Taiping and other rebels.

In both the Han and Qing, the interface of government with society was powerfully affected (in a positive way, usually) by official recruitment. The recruitment of new men into government, and the means by which it was done, was an absolutely central issue in 150 and 1850 and at all times in between. Recruitment was no simple matter of hiring and staffing. The government was everyone's employer of choice. Government office was a young man's only sure portal to fame and fortune. Even a weak central government was in a position to control levers determining which men, out of a huge press of candidates, were qualified to hold official positions. Down through all the centuries of China's history, various recruitment channels were made available, from purchase and inheritance, to the more prestigious and competitive ones: recommendation, and from Song times especially, written examinations. In 150, the Han central government relied mostly upon an elaborate system of recommendations, with mainly regional (commandery) officials responsible for recommending a given number of local men annually (the number depending upon the size of the commandery population), using as criteria good character and administrative ability, the latter usually tested by way of probationary assignment. Recommendation appears to have worked very well, but by around 150, intense rivalries at the highest levels in the capital introduced factionalism and corruption into the system.

In 1850, it was of course the national written examination system that had long eclipsed (in prestige, not numbers) all other modes of bureaucratic recruitment. A colossal industry produced, as reliably as clockwork, every third year a harvest of some 1,300 provincial degree winners (*juren*) and 300 metropolitan and palace degree winners (*jinshi*) out of a massive pool of around 90,000 classically educated eligible men who were themselves but a tiny fraction of the millions of local (county and prefectural) licentiates. What Han recruitment by recommendation did not do well, but the Qing examination system did, was to serve not just as a mechanism for filling official positions but also as a means for creating and sustaining a national society of educated local gentry without office but with fiscal and legal privileges and elite status.

Both the Han and the Qing, as central governments sensitive to the need to sustain unity over a very large territory, devised regional quotas to ensure that men from all parts of that territory had roughly equal chances to participate in the recruitment processes. Society itself would not have been so fair-minded. That central imperial authority played the vital role in ensuring distributive fairness is evident at many junctures, perhaps most dramatically in early Ming: In 1397, the examiners who were southerners awarded *jinshi* degrees to fifty-two men, all of them southerners. On strict grounds of merit, such a result might have been justified, because southerners had economic, cultural, and educational advantages that the northerners lacked. But the Ming founder reacted in fury, executing several of the graders. He ordered another exam. This one awarded degrees to sixty-one northerners. Thereafter, quotas guaranteed that, despite deficiencies, northerners would never again be excluded.

Pondering China and its ruling profile over a period of 1,700 years inevitably raises the question of the ideal and often the reality of political unity, and of just how the imperial state acted to maintain that unity. Political unity was not solely, or even mainly, seen as imposed by force—by the army and police, essential as those were. That there should be only one overarching governing structure encompassing all territory inhabited by people who spoke some form of Chinese, and were culturally Chinese in other ways, was early on anchored in the cosmic theory developed in that culture. Theory posited a known universe consisting of a triad of Heaven, Earth, and Humankind, with the emperor ("Son of Heaven") answerable to Heaven for the well-being of all the people, and Heaven responding with favorable or unfavorable portents. With the help of first one, then another, of the five cyclic powers (fire, metal, water, wood, and earth), Heaven delivered its mandate to good rulers and withdrew it from bad ones. This idea was more powerful in the Han than in the Qing. Over the very long term, the cosmic idea came to be doubted and partly discredited, though it was too useful ever to fade from political discourse completely.

The cosmic idea was not restricted to process. It permeated people's thoughts of structure as well. Indeed, hierarchy, the implicit framework upon which almost all complex structures hang, was according to inherited Confucian theory written into both the visible cosmos and human society. The subordination of moon to sun, of foreigners to Chinese, of child to parent, of younger brother to older, of wife to husband, of higher officials to lower, of all officials to ruler, and of ruler to Heaven was no arbitrary arrangement, but an invariable principle of nature. People of course often behave in unfilial or rebellious ways (government existed to encourage good behavior and repress bad), but seldom was it possible seriously to challenge the idea of hierarchy. In the absence or collapse of hierarchy in human systems, chaos (*luan*) was the usual awful result. The founder of the Ming dynasty, who early in his life had been involved with the antinomian Red Turban rebellion of the 1350s, later recalled that he saw how people of all classes, rich and poor, at first joined that rebellion against the Mongol Yuan dynasty in hope of raising their fame and status, or simply from an irresponsible love of disorder, only to discover that even rebel movements need elites of talent and leadership, and thus found themselves much worse off than they were before.

Society needed hierarchy for its own survival, and China preferred political unity for related reasons. Why unity was desirable was explicitly discussed by several south China literati in the Yuan-Ming interregnum of the mid-fourteenth century. Liu Ji, for one, argued that disunity was contagious because it was a license for every sort of corrupt evil; a disunited China, even a decentralized China, was a China ruled by the worst kinds of unsupervised local adventurers and thieves. But the whole period from 150 to 1850 shows that "China" in fact muddled through long periods when political disunion prevailed and prolonged interior warfare created repeated scenes of bloodshed and destruction. At such times, educated literati preserved the unifying ideals in written history, classical commentary, or literature, offered advice based on those ideals to warlords and local rulers, and perhaps put the ideals into practice at the levels of locality or family. So one finds the development of a near religion of Confucian filial piety, replete with stories of martyrs and miracles, during the post-Han centuries of political fragmentation, when effective ways were sought to strengthen family hierarchy, even at a time when it was Buddhism that best explained the universe and, together with Daoism, provided institutional support and psychic comfort in almost every part of the once-united realm. Or, in the politically broken world of twelfth-century China, the fathers of the Neo-Confucian (*daoxue*) movement of south China, frustrated with court politics, created their own hierarchies of masters and disciples and, largely circumventing the central state, experimented with autonomous local institutions to provide education, famine relief, and security.

It was only reasonable that theory should require that a unified Chinese state should come under a ruling house of ethnic Chinese origin, and yet a unified "China" managed somehow to carry on even under Mongol and later Manchu rule. The Chinese state carried on because it was possible to argue that virtue and capability always trumped ethnicity—that Heaven, casting about impartially for a worthy candidate to rule China, might well discover its man outside China altogether, in Mongolia or Manchuria. So the Chinese founder of the Ming dynasty reasoned about the Mongol Yuan that he had just destroyed: No doubt Heaven had given Chinggis Khan and his successors its mandate to rule China, but at the same time it was also clear that it should never have been Mongols ruling Chinese.

That was like wearing shoes on one's head and hats on one's feet. Worse, they never truly understood China's Confucian ideals, and in the end they proved incompetent to handle the tasks they had taken on. The Manchus rested their right to rule China on their virtues and capabilities, and they severely repressed any among the Chinese who called their ethnic credentials into question. The Yongzheng emperor went so far as to bring a Chinese critic and would-be organizer of an anti-Manchu rebellion named Zeng Jing to Beijing, had him observe for himself how orthodox and well-run Qing government was, and then published for general distribution a detailed refutation of Zeng's now recanted and discredited earlier views. (In 1736, however, the young Qianlong emperor thought his father had been scandalously lenient and had the hapless Zeng executed).

Thus "China" managed to survive many centuries of political anomaly. Yet the facts showed that having ethnic Chinese for one's rulers was not necessarily a blessing either. The last century and a half of Ming rule features five successive emperors whose pattern of behavior ranged from the capricious and bizarre to the monstrously extravagant and cruel. Officials criticized those emperors, but they did so at the risk of their careers and even their lives. The burst of great fiction writing in late Ming times centered upon rulers from history or other figures in positions of authority who, with their relentless stupidity, arbitrary brutality, and heedless self-absorption seem to have served as surrogates for the actual rulers of late Ming. Yet the power and influence of the Ming center was such that by their behavior the emperors unintentionally set models and examples for the rest of the realm. If emperors could act as they pleased, so might other people. Breaking the bonds of Confucian orthodoxy, ignoring master-disciple hierarchies, granting a measure of legitimacy to commonplace greed, and endorsing the passionate pursuit of one's heartfelt desires, whatever those might be, became the new direction taken by some leading scholar-officials and literati, including Lü Kun (1536–1618) and such seventeenth-century esthetes as Qi Biaojia (1602–1645), Zhang Dai (1597–at least 1684), and Wen Zhenheng (1585–1645).

Between the imperial court above and the local officials ministering to millions of people below, there was sandwiched the intricate machinery of central and regional government, staffed mainly by

Confucian-trained mandarins, who were the custodians and supervisors of routine administration and simultaneously articulate spokesmen for what was sometimes called the "national right" (*guo shi*), which is to say they aimed to be constructive critics of erring rulers and of ongoing high policy. Those were two very different roles, difficult for single individuals or government departments to keep in balance. The one role stemmed from Legalist theory, the other from Confucian.

The routine of government, as embodied in its array of central offices, did not change fundamentally over the years 150 to 1850. The topmost (prime ministerial) organs showed some change, however. At times the prime ministerial function lay in the hands of one individual (in 1380, Ming Taizu abolished that arrangement for all time); at other times, the function was divided between two or more men. In 150 there was a grand commandant with a large array of supervisory bureaus under his control, but he was also but one of a troika of high officials, with whom he shared censorial and advisory duties. Below the troika sat the "nine ministers," each with special functions and each with large staffs, not controlled by the troika, but subject to its oversight. One main difference between the Nine Ministries of the Later Han and the analogous Six Ministries of the Qing was that the former included palace functions and the latter did not. But Rites, Justice, Revenue, and War were ministries common to both. The Qing also had ministries for personnel and public works.

A torrent of documents coursed through both governments: reports, impeachments, and advice rising upward, and imperial edicts, judicial decisions, directives, and other pronouncements flowing downward. In Later Han, a large Imperial Secretariat handled most of the documentary traffic. In Qing, which is known in extraordinary detail, a sophisticated system of paper flow after 1736 divided official business into routine and nonroutine, with a new body, the Grand Council, handling the latter with remarkable efficiency and speed.

Later Han central government consisted of a large and confusing agglomeration of offices; by contrast, Qing central government appears rational and streamlined, with palace functions clearly separated from the rest. Both governments established ranking systems for officials—the Han based on salary, the Qing on a numerical scale of eighteen grades. Rivalrous imperial distaff families and palace eunuchs participated in Later Han government; in the Qing, these elements had been all but disenfranchised. Both governments can be described as meritocracies, as officials were regularly supervised, assessed, and reported upon, and were promoted or punished accordingly. The censorial functions of remonstrance, impeachment, and surveillance (a notable part of almost all of China's historical governments) were diffuse and decentralized in the Later Han, with the result that late in that period, provincial-level officials had little difficulty turning themselves into autonomous warlords. In the Qing, the system of provincial governors, governors-general, and circuit intendants, with divided and overlapping duties, helped protect central authority from that sort of breakdown. As concerns military institutions, retrospectively one can see that the years 150 and 1850 were late in the history of both regimes, and their once-powerful military systems were in decline. The national draft of the Han had eroded, northern border defense had been subcontracted to various Inner Asian tribes, and local landed magnates were more and more left to provide for their own security. Likewise, the Qing "Banner" system of hereditary Manchu, Mongol, and Chinese forces had weakened; and as the Han had had to rely on new armies to deal with the Yellow Turbans, so too the Qing had to allow the recruitment of new regional armies to deal with the Taiping and other rebellions. Whereas in both instances the rebels were defeated, neither dynasty was able fully to recoup central authority in the aftermath of the suppression. The Han fell soon after, but the Qing managed much better to retain the loyalty of the commanders of the new regional armies.

On balance, then, Qing China was culturally as well as institutionally not all that far removed from Later Han China. Han history was full of useful examples, and students, scholars, and scholar-officials in Qing times regularly studied it. Indeed, it was Han historians who created the model for organizing and writing dynastic history, a model faithfully followed in later times, down to the Qing publication of the Ming dynastic history in 1739, and of the Qing dynastic history by the Republic in Taipei in 1962. Between 150 and 1850, no challenge was threatening enough to prompt a complete institutional remodeling of the country. Gunpowder weapons, invented in China in the thirteenth century, and reintroduced in improved form by the Portuguese in the sixteenth and seventeenth centuries, failed to have the dramatic impact in China that they had had in late medieval Europe. At the very same time, unprecedented quantities of Japanese and South American silver poured into China in exchange for huge shipments of silk and porcelain, and this did cause some significant economic and fiscal changes, but never enough to call the whole inherited institutional apparatus into question. The structural soundness of it all is striking. China's was a simple system, really: small governments, usually dedicated to downsizing and tax reduction; grounded in Confucian and Legalist doctrines that were, at least on the surface, easy to understand and hard to challenge; and reasonably effective in providing such foundational public goods as security (*an*) and good order (*zhi*).

The 1,700 years of recorded history that lie between 150 and 1850 show that as the centuries wore on, slow but visible progress was made in refining the tools of a unified political system. There took place a continual re-engineering of the dynastic system, such that the Ming and Qing, as compared to earlier dynasties, achieved an unusually high level of internal stability and unity. Changes occurred in response to serious challenges. As Liu Ji remarked in the fourteenth century, new dynasties may be institutionally tailored to overcome a current set of problems, only to encounter a set of new and unanticipated problems that require new policies and approaches for their solution. It is this feature of history that lends compelling interest to all of China's past, not just to the more recent parts of it.

It seems convenient to divide this very long historical record into several smaller segments of time during which the wielders of power over China's landscape dealt, successfully and unsuccessfully, with the big problems of the times. I have singled out four such segments in this book. First is the long age of fragmentation and disorder that begins with the Han collapse in 221 and extends to the Sui reunification in 589. The second deals with the golden age of empire that encompasses the Sui and Tang down to the An Lushan rebellion of 755 and continues into the long postimperial period of increasing disorder and disunion that lasted to the formal end of Tang rule in 907. The third segment covers the years 907 to 1279, nearly four centuries during which the government of "China" was divided among the Five Dynasties and Ten Kingdoms (907–975), then fell short of complete reunification, as first the Liao then the Jin ruled in the north, the Xi Xia ruled in the extreme west, and the Northern and then the Southern Song ruled in the center and south. This appeared to be a permanent tripartition of mainland East Asia. In something of a surprise move, an external force, the Mongols, reunified China in 1279. Like the period 221–589, the period 907–1279 featured innovation in many fields: technological, intellectual, and political. The final segment takes us from 1279 to 1850, a coherent unit of time insofar as the Mongol Yuan unification of China established a legacy of unity and stability that with a few relatively brief interruptions has continued down to modern times. The book ends in 1850, on the eve of the great rebellions that, in conjunction with the increasing pressures of the industrializing West, eventually led to the ruin of the Qing, as well as the whole inherited dynastic tradition along with it, in the early part of the twentieth century.

The governing of China had two very different aspects. One was structural, bureaucratic, rational, usually orderly and predictable, and slow to change. The other was emotional and volatile, a playground for rivalry, ambition, fear, greed, shortsightedness, stupidity, factionalism, partisan zealotry, and corruption. There was always dynamic interplay between these two aspects of governance. Both rode on a substratum of society at large as well as the productive resources that the people of China wrung from the landscape. People and resources grew and shrank and changed over time, with consequences for both aspects of governance. It all makes for an absorbing story.

Timelines

1. An Age of Disunion

The fragile, short-lived, and mainly regional northern dynasties of this era are difficult to plot on timelines or maps. Many of their names, however, are ancient names for regional states during China's Zhou era (1100–256 BCE), and thus it may be noted that the various Yan dynasties originated in the northeast, the various Jin, Zhao, and Wei dynasties in north-central China, the Qin dynasties and the Zhou in the west, and the various Shu regimes in Sichuan. The term "Six Dynasties" (not used in this book) refers to south China, from the Wu dynasty down to the Chen.

Later Han, 25–220
    Failed massacre of palace eunuchs, 168
    Yellow Turban rebellion, 184
    Rule of Cao Cao, 196–220
        Cao Cao's defeat at Red Cliffs on the Yangzi, 208
The Three Kingdoms, 221–264
Cao-Wei, 221–266   Shu-Han, 221–264   Wu, 229–280
Western Jin, 266–311
    War of the Eight Princes, 301–307
    Liu Cong destroys Luoyang, 311
Latter Zhao, 330–349   Eastern Jin, 318–420
    Shi Le, r. 330–333
    Shi Hu, r. 333–349
    Ran Min (Wei dynasty), r. 349–352
Former Yan, 353–370
Former Qin, 370–383
    Former Qin defeated by Eastern Jin at Battle
    of the Fei River, 383
Northern Wei, 398–534   Liu-Song, 420–477
    North China reunified, 450   Qi, 479–501
    Revolt of the Six Garrisons, 523–534   Liang, 502–556
Western Wei, 534–550; Eastern Wei, 534–557
Chen, 557–587

Northern Zhou, 557–581; Northern Qi, 550–577
   Northern Zhou reunifies north China and Sichuan, 577
   Sui founded, 581

2. Imperial Grandeur
Sui, 581–618
   Wendi, r. 581–604
      China fully reunified, 589
   Yangdi, r. 604–618
Tang, 618–907
   Taizu (Li Yuan), r. 618–626
   Taizong (Li Shimin), r. 626–649
   Empress Wu, in power 655–705
   Xuanzong, r. 712–756
      An Lushan rebellion, 755–763
   Wuzong, r. 840–846
   Suppression of Buddhism, 845–846
Huang Chao rebellion, 875–884
Five Dynasties and Ten Kingdoms, 907–960 (975)

3. The Tripartition of China
Liao (927–1125) Northern Song (960–1126) Xi Xia (982–1227)
   Liao acquires the sixteen north China prefectures, 937
   Zhao Kuangyin (also called Song Taizu), r. 960–976
   Treaty of Shanyuan, 1004
   Wang Anshi in power, 1067–1085
   Huizong, r. 1100–1125
   Jin dynasty declared, 1115 (to 1234)
      Jin conquest of Kaifeng, 1127
   Southern Song founded, 1127
      Treaties between Jin and Song, 1142, 1165, 1208
      Zhu Xi Neo-Confucianism made state orthodoxy, 1240
      Jia Sidao as Southern Song chief minister, 1259–1275
      Fall of Hangzhou, Southern Song court surrenders
      to the Mongols, 1276
      Last remnants of the Southern Song destroyed, 1279

4. Permanent Unity Achieved
Yuan, 1271–1368
   Khubilai, r. 1260–1294

Confucian examination system restored, 1315
Yellow River rerouted, 1351
Red Turban rebellions, 1351–1354
Chancellor Toghto dismissed, 1355
Yuan breakup and civil war, 1355–1368
Ming, 1368–1644
   Taizu (Zhu Yuanzhang), r. 1368–1398
   Prime minister's position abolished, 1380
   Yongle (Zhu Di), r. 1402–1424
      Voyages of Zheng He, 1405–1433
      Invasions of Mongolia, 1410–1424
      Ming capital moved to Beijing, 1421
      Vietnam occupation, 1406–1427
   Zhengtong emperor captured by Mongols, 1449
   Jiajing reign, 1522–1566
   Wanli reign, 1572–1620
      Grand Secretary Zhang Juzheng in power, 1572–1582
      Matteo Ricci in China, 1583–1610
      Wars in Korea, 1593, 1597
   Eunuch Wei Zhongxian in power, 1624–1627
   Revolts of Li Zicheng and Zhang Xianzhong, from 1628
      Li (Shun dynasty) occupies Beijing, 1644
      Suicide of Chongzhen, last Ming emperor, 1644
Qing China (1644 to 1850)
   Shunzhi, r. 1643–1661   Southern Ming, 1644–1659
   Kangxi, r. 1661–1722
      War of the Three Feudatories, 1673–1681
      Conquest of Taiwan, 1683
      Treaty of Nerchinsk, 1689
      Defeat of the Zunghars, 1697
      Conquest of Tibet, 1720
   Yongzheng, r. 1722–1735
   Qianlong, r. 1735–1799
      Creation of Grand Council, 1736
      Extermination of the Zunghars, 1757
      Annexation of Eastern Turkestan (Xinjiang), 1765
      Hešen, in power 1775–1799
   Jiaqing, r. 1796 (1799)–1820
   Daoguang, r. 1820–1850

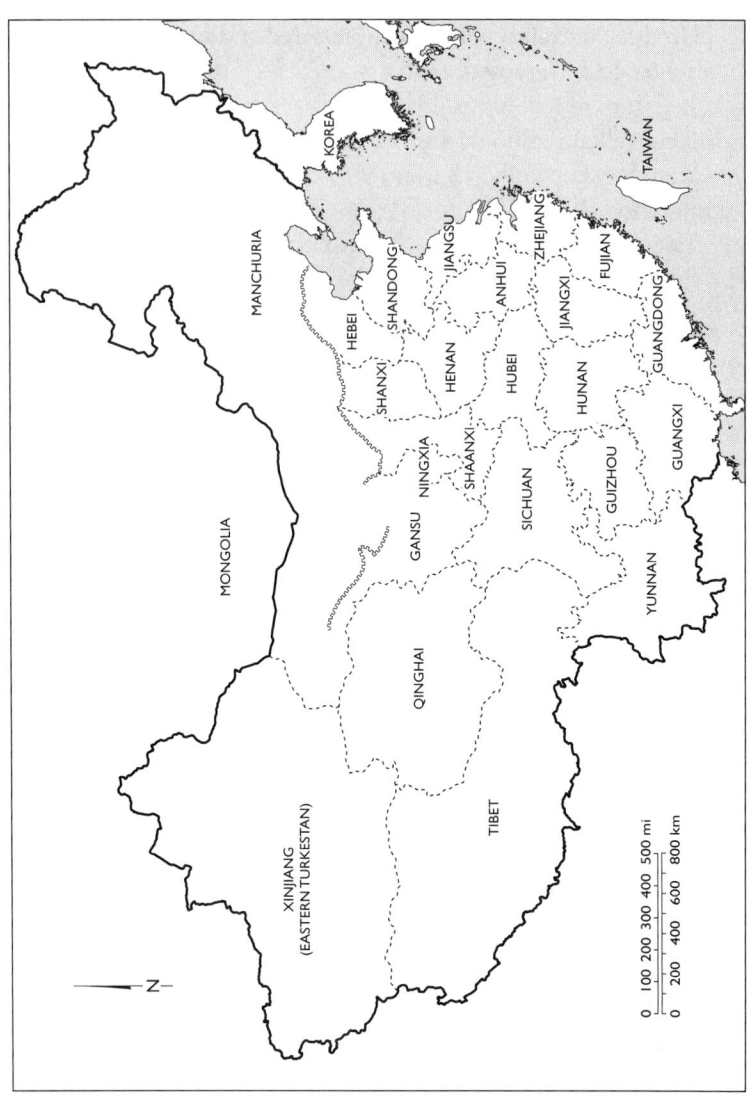

Map 1. Provinces and regions of present-day China.

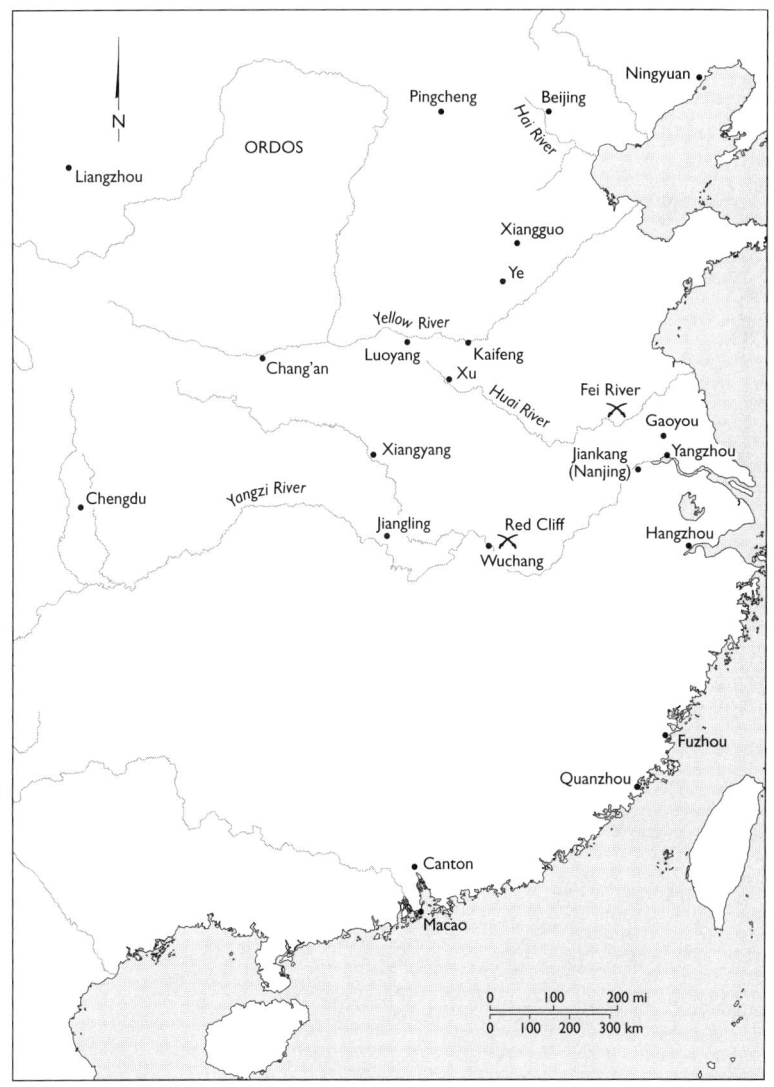

Map 2. Place-names mentioned in the text.

Part I

From Fragmentation to Reunification 150–589

Unprecedented turmoil troubled the four and a half centuries from 150 on. There was the breakdown of the Han; then the three-way split of power that followed; then a short-lived reassembly of the broken pieces under the Western Jin (266–311); then an extreme splintering, featuring many competing regimes; and finally the piecemeal construction of a new central system that was once again capable of reuniting the country and providing it with security and order. There is no exaggerating the suffering that all of this political turmoil spread in its wake: the roving armies and militias, with their burning, looting, and massacres; the famines; the enserfments, enslavements, and mass migrations both voluntary and forced. It is no accident that the legend of Peach Blossom Spring, where for centuries a happy society of peasants were said to have lived in seclusion, shielded from all the post-Han upheavals, took final shape under the pen of Tao Qian, whose life spanned the years 365 to 427, right in the middle of those disordered times.

The problems that had to be solved before a unified realm could be reconstituted were too many and too difficult to be solved all at once. In north China, the mainly Inner Asian rulers and their advisers needed to find ways to get Inner Asian and Chinese elites to cooperate; to integrate Inner Asian and Chinese armies; and to create a resource base sufficient to support central armies powerful enough to overcome Chinese local magnates with their private estates and militias as well as hostile Inner Asian frontier tribes. It complicated matters that there had grown and spread the Daoist and Buddhist religions, which could either oppose dynastic rule or collaborate and help strengthen it. South China's dynastic states meanwhile did little to lay groundwork for reunification. North China's regimes did all the work. However, for centuries, stability in the north seemed beyond reach. But from about 450, the Northern Wei dynasty began to lay important institutional foundations, which their successors retained and improved upon. From then on, the advance toward empire began to gather speed, such that the reunification, when it came about in 589 with the Sui extinction of the last southern regime, seems in retrospect almost unaccountably sudden.

The era of fragmentation, aside from the destructiveness of all its wars, also featured court-centered political violence of extraordinary proportions. In both north and south China, royal murders and palace massacres were almost a commonplace component of factional infighting at the highest levels. Away from court, many of the educated elites of south China (there were few of them in the north) tried to avoid the dangers of government and instead occupied themselves with literature, religion, and family matters. Elites insisted on drawing a hard distinction between themselves as an upper class with deep genealogical credentials and the mass of ordinary people who lacked them. That distinction would blur in future times. What is notable about this era is the blurring of what would in the future become rigidly differentiated. The age of fragmentation featured strong intermingling at the top of the social, political, and military hierarchies. Members of the best families were among those who founded dynasties. Socially high-ranking families married their daughters to the emperors. The emperor's relatives held many of the highest military and political positions. Men often held civil and military posts concurrently. Likewise there was no clear dividing line between palace positions and positions in the outer bureaucracy. All of this blurring would end in later times.

The years from 150 to 589 were not unrelievedly dismal, however. This was a time for innovation. This was a time when Buddhism spread through China north and south, bringing with it new ways of thinking about life and death, as well as temples endowed with land and other resources that helped promote economic redevelopment in the countryside and pioneered such new institutions as orphanages, pawnshops, auctions, as well as roads, bridges, inns, and other facilities for travelers. In south China, elite émigrés from the north produced a formidable body of new literature that would come to constitute a major cultural legacy in Tang and later times. But let us now look at this age of disunion and its resolution in greater detail.

The Unraveling of the Later Han 150–220

For more than four hundred years, the principal East Asian power was, by every relevant index, China's Han dynasty (206 BCE–220 CE). It ruled some fifty million people living mainly in the northern parts of what is now commonly called "China proper." The capital was Luoyang, which encompassed an area slightly less than half the size of Manhattan, and at some five hundred thousand inhabitants may have been the largest city in the world of its time. In fact, of the fourteen largest cities in the world, nine were Chinese. Led by hereditary monarchs of the Liu family, the realm was administered by a ranked and salaried bureaucracy, which through a hierarchy of prefectures and counties exerted a high degree of control over the country at large.

But by the latter part of the second century, a long era of prosperity had ended and the regime was clearly in trouble. At the center, in Luoyang, a complex power struggle among the civil officials, the imperial in-law families, and the large corps of palace eunuchs led in 168 to the exposure of a plot to massacre the eunuchs, followed at once by the eunuchs' retaliatory purge of everyone even remotely involved. This purge had serious consequences. Those purged prided themselves as a "pure" group, bonded together by ties of ethical learning and altruistic motives. In exile they took up "pure conversation" as free intellectuals, making pure moral judgments (*qingyi*) of men and affairs. The effect of this on the fate of the Han is hard to gauge, but in the end it can be said that the best and brightest of China's intelligentsia were not motivated to rally to the dynasty's support.

In the countryside at large, a Han government that earlier was adept at extending disaster relief gave up on it after about 100 CE

By the 150s, famine had created large bodies of starving drifters in the north China plains. This set the stage for a complete breakdown of the existing Han order. In the 170s, Daoist sectarians in thickly populated Shandong developed a vision of a post-Han utopia of Great Peace (*taiping*), while in Sichuan a deified Laozi revealed himself to an alchemist named Zhang Daoling, warned him of the approaching end of the world, and empowered him to recruit and lead a community of chosen people. This movement soon turned itself into an effective and self-regulated paragovernment. Distressed peasants turned to these sects, or to local magnates, for aid and protection, or turned to violence on their own. For several months in the spring and summer of 184, a cataclysm known as the Yellow Turban rebellion, led by the sectarian Zhang brothers (no relation to Zhang Daoling), raged across much of north China. It was crushed by the end of that year not by central forces, but by armies under the command of local and regional warlords only nominally loyal to the Han. Further struggle among the warlords brought about the complete massacre of the palace eunuchs in the same year, 184, and the capture by first one warlord, then another, of first one, then another young scion of the Han imperial family. Luoyang was looted and burned. By 196, the dominant northern warlord, the highly literate and capable Cao Cao, abandoned Luoyang for Xu, a prefecture some distance east. He placed the last Han emperor there and through him tried to rule China. Cao used a different city, Ye, as his own military headquarters.

Cao sought to create a new regime for China. He attracted to his cause literati who had long been alienated from the Han. He built a new government using a new recruitment mechanism, the "Nine Ranks and Impartial Judges" system, which put the literati and their "pure opinions" to use weighing the talents and virtues of the recruits. He set up military and civilian plantations for defeated troops and refugees, allocating them lands, and putting their labor and taxable crops to use by the central state. He brought the Gongsun warlords of southern Manchuria to heel, and, in Liangzhou in the far west, he ended a sixty-year rising by frontier generals of the Qiang people. Trade connections with Central Asia and India were then reopened. In 216, an independent Daoist state in northeast Sichuan peacefully surrendered to him. However, these efforts at reunification were perhaps too far ahead of their time, and Cao too advanced in years to sustain them. In 208, in the famous Red Cliffs encounter, the warlords Liu Bei in Sichuan and Sun Quan on the lower Yangzi River joined naval forces and foiled Cao's attack. He never attempted another.

A few months after Cao Cao's death, his eldest son and successor, Cao Pi, under the guidance of the best ritual experts of the time, arranged for the peaceful abdication of the last Han emperor and the transfer of the heavenly mandate to a new dynasty, the Wei, with himself as its first emperor, wrapped in the aura of a Daoist sage. A partially rebuilt Luoyang was his capital. Warlord Liu (who asserted kinship with the Han imperial house) broke away and declared his own legitimist Shu-Han dynasty in Sichuan in 221. The warlord Sun founded a Wu dynasty in 229, with its capital first at Wuchang (now Echeng county, Hubei) on the mid-Yangzi and later downstream at Jiankang (now Nanjing). Thus began the so-called Three Kingdoms era, immortalized in the famous Ming novel *Romance of the Three Kingdoms*, with its intriguing opening thesis—"They say that the realm has a strong tendency to unite after a long period of disunion, and after a long period of unity, to divide."

The Three Kingdoms 221–264

Shu-Han was the smallest and weakest component of tripartite China, despite the charismatic presence and administrative talents of its chief official, Zhuge Liang (d. 234). In 264, Shu-Han was conquered and annexed by Wei. The Shu-Han regime's most famous scholar and man of letters, Qiao Zhou, helped negotiate favorable treatment for both his ruler and himself.

The Wu empire was territorially as large as the Wei, but it had a much smaller population, as the lands south of the Huai and Yangzi rivers were filling up only slowly with Chinese-speaking settlers. The Sun family, founders of the Wu state, were native southerners of undistinguished pedigree. Though administratively weak, and never able to carry out a proper census, Wu was geographically coherent and economically well-off, and it successfully defended itself until conquered from the north in 280.

The Cao-Wei regime, by far the largest of the Three Kingdoms in population and resources, was gradually subverted from within by succeeding generations of the exceptionally powerful Sima family. Sima Yi (179–251), his sons Shi and Zhao, and his grandson Yan (236–290) reduced the Cao emperors to ciphers, much as Cao Cao had earlier done with the Han. The realm was also vexed along its entire northern frontier by non-Chinese peoples, some nomadic and some not, over whom the Cao-Wei struggled to impose a degree of hegemony. Such groups as the Yuwen and Murong in the northeast, the Tuoba directly north, the Xiongnu in southern Shanxi, and the Tuyuhun in the far west seem to have been Turco-Mongolian speakers. Near neighbors of the Tuyuhun were the Di and the Qiang, speakers of languages apparently related to Tibetan. All these border peoples would play major military and political roles in north China in the coming years.

The Western Jin
266–311

In the same way that Cao Pi deposed the last Han emperor in 221, so in turn, on February 8, 266, Sima Yan deposed the last Cao-Wei ruler and made himself founding emperor of a new dynasty called the Jin. (Later, it was referred to as the Western Jin.)

The Jin introduced some important policy changes, including especially a strong tendency to disfavor obscure men of talent (whom Cao Cao had tried to recruit through the Impartial Judges system), and instead to cultivate the support and encourage the participation in government of men from powerful families of established pedigree. Sima Yan favored his own powerful family as well. Some fifty-seven princedoms were set up for Sima family members. Each controlled armies. Some five hundred smaller fiefdoms, carefully graded, were created as hereditary holdings for other powerful supporters of the Sima. The main goal for the new regime was reunification. A well-planned campaign against the Wu realm featured a six-pronged assault, with five armies attacking from the north while a flotilla organized up the Yangzi in Sichuan attacked from the west. Weakened by internal strife, horrific palace murders, and major defections to the enemy, the last Wu emperor surrendered on May 31, 280, and his realm was annexed to the Jin. China was reunified. But not for long.

Hardly was China reunified when it began to descend into a maelstrom of violence and even worse disintegration than that occasioned by the fracture of the Han into the Three Kingdoms eighty years before.

Reunified China held together under the controlling hand of the first Jin emperor, Sima Yan. When he died in 290, however, his successor was his eldest surviving son, Sima Zhong (259–306), unfortunately mentally disabled. Fierce rivalry broke out between the Yang family of the new emperor's mother and the Jia family of his wife. Their struggle attracted the intervention of the Sima princes, holders of military and civil governorships as well as fiefs. In 291, a Sima prince conducted a slaughter of the Yang and their adherents. In 301, prompted by the murder of the heir apparent, another prince, Sima Lun, massacred the Jia family and declared himself emperor. That sparked the infamous "War of the Eight Princes" (301–307), which laid much of north China to waste, and indeed ended Jin rule there.

This fratricidal war focused first on Luoyang; but after 305, massacre, famine, and disease afflicted other cities, such as Chang'an, and much of the north China countryside. Refugees fled to the northeast, the northwest, and especially to the south.

In part of the northwest, the Li family, of non-Chinese (Ba) descent, led a mass migration of some two hundred thousand Daoist communitarians away from local violence and famine south to Sichuan, where in 302 Li Te founded a Cheng (later called Cheng-Han) dynasty. Elsewhere in the northwest, a local Chinese magnate named Zhang Gui (254–314) founded a (Former) Liang dynasty and established a haven for refugees from wars further east. In the far northeast, meanwhile, Murong Hui (d. 335) gradually built a Chinese-style administration, welcomed Chinese refugees, set up a Chinese school to educate his own family and select members of the tribal elite, and laid groundwork for future expansion. The formal declaration of a (Former) Yan empire would come about under a successor in 353. Thus bits first broke away from the Jin in its eastern and western extremities and in Sichuan. Worse followed. Xiongnu tribespeople, long settled in Shanxi as semisedentary horse breeders, found themselves drawn into the vortex of the War of the Eight Princes. The hereditary Xiongnu leader Liu Yuan had had a good Chinese education and had spent time in Luoyang in better days. One of the warring Sima princes enlisted his aid in the struggle. But Liu Yuan felt himself and his people disrespected and mistreated by the Jin. In 304, at his fort in central Shanxi, he declared his own Han dynasty. In 307 he conquered southern Shanxi. Two large bandit forces roving about the north China plain joined him the same year. One, consisting of Chinese refugees and displaced tribespeople, was commanded by Shi Le, a non-Chinese warlord with a major future role to play. Liu Yuan died of illness in the summer of 310, whereupon his brother Liu Cong, also well educated, murdered Liu Yuan's designated successor and seized power for himself. Liu Cong then destroyed Luoyang in a frightful bloodbath in 311. The Jin emperor fled, but was caught and put to death. So ended the so-called Western Jin.

A Fractured Age
311–450

The grand leitmotifs that shaped events in the foregoing, and in what follows, seem to be three in number. One is the very durable idea of the dynastic state, grounded in Legalist and Confucian theory, and best exemplified in the great Qin and Han regimes of the past. Knowledge of the ideas and the history was transmitted generation after generation through education, often family centered, and at times also religion based or state supported. The second is the importance of family and lineage for Chinese and non-Chinese alike. The potent combination of state and elite lineage, each needing the help of the other, seems to have prevented China from evolving into either a centralized despotism or, at the other extreme, a Polish-style feudalism. The third leitmotif is the high value everyone placed on Chinese education, Chinese texts, and Chinese literary mastery. Chinese and non-Chinese elites alike shared a rough agreement on all these important matters. Thus nothing like an all-out racial war pitting Chinese against non-Chinese ever took place, even though language differences, differences in clothing and customs, differences in hair color and facial characteristics, and perceived unequal treatment could kindle savage animosities from time to time, as noted previously, and as will be noted again later.

The period from 304 to 439 in north China, from Liu Yuan's declaring a Han dynasty down to the reunification of the north by the Northern Wei, is traditionally known as the period of the "Five Barbarians and Sixteen Kingdoms." Eighteen kingdoms would be more exact. The so-called Five Barbarians were the Xiongnu (under the rule of the Liu, Juqu, and Helian families); the Jie (the Shi family); the Xianbi (Murong, Tufa, Qifu, and later the Yuwen and Tuoba); the Di (Fu, Lü, and Yang families); and Qiang (Yao family). In the south, the Chinese Jin dynasty was restored and relocated by a regional prince, Sima Rui, at Jiankang on the Yangzi in 318. It is known as the Eastern Jin.

The last Xiongnu ruler of Liu Yuan's new Han dynasty, Liu Cong, died in 318. His cousin Liu Yao, who had conquered Guanzhong (the "Land within the Passes," now southern Shaanxi), thereupon declared a (Former) Zhao dynasty at Chang'an. Shi Le, warlord of the Jie people (their ethnic identities are not clear), earlier an adherent of Liu Yuan, then declared his own (Latter) Zhao dynasty at Xiangguo (near Ye, in southern Hebei). The two raced to seize Luoyang. Shi won and executed Liu in 329. In the year following, Shi assumed the title of emperor. Foreign warlord though he may have been, Shi favored schools, liked to have famous old Chinese texts read aloud to him, and had a few Chinese literati (such as Zhang Bin) as advisers. But of equal importance in advancing his career was his association with the non-Chinese Buddhist monk Fotudeng (also rendered as Fotucheng, d. 348 or 349) from Kucha in present-day Xinjiang. As a Buddhist convert and church patron, Shi helped introduce a new element to China—an officially sponsored and text-based higher religion that was neither Chinese nor "barbarian" and was thus able to minister equally to both. Fotudeng was also useful to Shi as a rainmaker, prognosticator, and political and military strategist. Additionally, he gathered about him many famous Central Asian and Chinese disciples who would carry on the work of evangelizing Buddhism in China.

Although Shi's Latter Zhao unified much of north China, the Murong clan continued to build its power in the extreme northeast, while in the extreme west, the Zhang family ruled autonomously. In Chouchi, a statelet squeezed between the Latter Zhao in Shaanxi and the Cheng-Han state in Sichuan, Yang Nandi (a "White Horse" Di) also ruled autonomously. All three regimes accepted the token suzerainty of the Eastern Jin at Jiankang. Early in 333, Shi himself sent a peace envoy to Jiankang.

But none of this presaged an imminent revival of peace, order, and unity. Shi died on August 17, 333. His nephew Shi Hu seized power and ruled violently but effectively until he died in 349. Three years of utter hell followed. Ran Min, a Chinese who was Shi Hu's adopted son and commander of his forces at Ye (the capital), slaughtered the entire Shi family and changed the name of the state to Wei. Then, calling on ethnic Chinese soldiers, he began a campaign of genocide against the Jie and other barbarians in and around Ye. Some two hundred thousand barbarians of both sexes and all ages are said to have been killed. Into this pit of horror advanced the armies of Murong Jun from the northeast, their way prepared by propaganda of saving the people from Ran. Murong's cavalry defeated Ran's infantry, and on June 1, 352, Ran himself was captured and executed. A siege of Ye followed. It fell on September 8. Exactly what prompted Ran's personal and racial hatreds is unfortunately obscure.

The Murong invasion of north-central China seemed to promise peace under a stable and relatively well-ordered regime. Urged on by Chinese advisers, Murong declared himself emperor of the (Former) Yan dynasty on January 4, 353. Five years later, he moved his capital southwest to Ye. Preparations were afoot to conduct a major campaign into the far west and so to unify north China under Yan rule. But Murong died in 360, leaving a very young successor and uncertainties in top leadership. Then came severe famines, forcing a postponement of the campaign. In 370, the Former Yan was destroyed by an invasion from the far west. The invader, Fu Jian, would try his own hand at unifying not just north China, but the south as well.

Why were these early hybrid regimes, composed of barbarians and Chinese, so fragile? Institutionally, military power dominated everything else, with the partial exception of an emerging Buddhist church. A major defeat of an army often led at once to the destruction of the state that sponsored it. Both Chinese and non-Chinese were enrolled into armies, but as Ran Min's acts showed, mutual hostilities were not hard to provoke. Nor were the various barbarian armies necessarily friendly with one another. An army led by the ruler, his family members, and close followers tended (when not on campaign) to be concentrated around the ruler's fort or capital, walled towns such as Xiangguo or Ye, and there was little permanent deployment of forces beyond there.

Precious little is known of civil administration, tax-assessing, or tax collection. Trade was precarious, agriculture insecure. The Chinese-settled parts of north China seem to have been peppered with small defensive forts in which rural inhabitants might from time to time find protection under the hereditary local strongmen who built them. For the rulers of states, manpower shortage was clearly a problem. Wars were fought as much to acquire people as to occupy land. One regularly reads of Chinese and barbarian captives being forcibly moved in the tens of thousands, usually to the ruler's capital region. Then when the state collapsed, many of these captives would migrate back to whence they came. Commanders and their armies in the field, Chinese and barbarian, occasionally defected en masse to the Eastern Jin regime in the south. Disorders propelled many Chinese, perhaps two million in all, to emigrate from north China altogether and seek new lives in the south. Northern regimes could scarcely cope with all the difficulties.

After the Former Yan failure, the next would-be unifier was Fu Jian, leader of the Di people of the far west and founder of the (Former) Qin empire. Fu managed to press together a huge but loose coalition of people and their commanders and articulate a clear purpose—to bring Buddhist salvation to all and rescue humankind from the troubles. In 383, a combined Former Qin force said to number two hundred seventy thousand horsemen and six hundred thousand infantry began a southeastward assault across the Huai. Incredibly, and for reasons that are now obscure, it was there stopped by an Eastern

Jin counterattack. (This was the famous Battle of the Fei River, a tributary of the Huai, at a site no longer identifiable, due to the hydrographic rearrangements made by man and nature since that time.) Almost at once, the Former Qin state broke apart. Murong Chui declared independence under a (Later) Yan dynasty (384–408). Another Murong declared a (Western) Yan in central Shanxi and Guanzhong (384–396). Yao Chang, leader of the Qiang people, put Fu Jian to death near Chang'an in 385 and founded the (Later) Qin dynasty (384–417). Lü Guang, a Di commander earlier sent by Fu to conquer Xinjiang (and capture the famous Buddhist monk and translator Kumārajīva from Kucha) set up his own (Later) Liang dynasty (386–403) in Gansu. But by far the most important piece of the Former Qin to declare independence was the Dai regime, later the Northern Wei, of the Tuoba tribe of Xianbi, based close to the steppes in northern Shanxi.

Unity in the North: The Northern Wei 398–534

The Northern Wei rulers conquered bit by bit the fragments of the collapsed Former Qin and by the year 450 achieved the military unification of north China. By force, luck, and some constructive achievements in administration and policy, the Northern Wei managed to postpone its own collapse until the year 534. This represented a great leap upward in the strengthening of the northern system of rule. Important groundwork was laid for the Sui and Tang reunifications many years later.

The Northern Wei is famous for its colossal Buddhist statuary, first carved at Yungang in the vicinity of Pingcheng, an early capital in far northern Shanxi. The city of Pingcheng itself was a monument to what sheer compulsion could accomplish. Conquered peoples by the tens of thousands were, over many years, forced to relocate there in order to raise crops, tend cattle and horses, and live within the walls of the city, which was planned, built by forced labor, and divided into a palace quarter, residential wards, markets, and slave-manned workshops for weapons, woolen and silk manufacture, brewing, and the like. The whole was heavily policed. Pingcheng was like an overgrown military or prison camp.

Eager to harness spiritual power to the dynastic cause and facilitate a shift from tribalism to autocracy, the Northern Wei emperor Taiwu interrupted his predecessors' preoccupations with Buddhism to take up during the years 425 to 450 a flirtation with the Chinese Daoist church, a descendant of the theocracy created in Sichuan in the second century, as noted earlier. The church's "celestial master," Kou Qianzhi, received a divine revelation that Taiwu was destined to become a "perfect ruler of Great Peace." Kou's chief disciple, Cui Hao (381–450), served Taiwu as Fotudeng had earlier served Shi Le, but did much more: besides prognosticating and strategizing as the Kuchean Fotudeng had done, the Chinese Cui also became prime minister and virtual ruler, directing the growth of an official Daoist church and to some extent remodeling Northern Wei government so as to bring it in line with a long-standing Daoist dream (based on vague information about the Roman Empire) of a utopia anchored in peace, justice, and ritual order.

A major rebellion of peoples—Chinese, Di, Qiang, and Xiongnu—erupted in Guanzhong (southern Shaanxi) in 448. Emperor Taiwu personally led the forces that put this down. Discovering that Buddhist monks had been heavily involved in the rising, Taiwu began an empire-wide suppression of that faith. The official Daoist church was text-based and elitist, whereas Buddhism had begun to make converts among the common people of the Chinese villages and the tribal settlements. Dissident monks had been involved in not just this, but also several other eschatological movements against the Northern Wei government. The suppression was short-lived. The Daoist church's extraordinary hegemony ended with Kou's death in 448, the execution of Cui and his adherents in 450, and the assassination of Taiwu himself in 452. Buddhism then returned to favor, and the Northern Wei drive toward autocracy was dampened a bit until 490.

From 465 to 490, Dowager Empress Feng presided over an astoundingly active phase of Northern Wei history. She was the part-Chinese, part-Xianbi granddaughter of the last emperor of the brief Northern Yan dynasty of Liaodong. Her father defected with his family to the Northern Wei; after his execution, she was put in the harem, and from there she rose to power on the basis of her own vigor, passion, and manipulative skills. She resumed the carving of the Buddha statues at Yungang, with the Buddhas made to resemble the earlier Northern Wei rulers, who were now considered reincarnated Buddhas themselves. She built monasteries and pagodas in Pingcheng, which by 476 had some hundred structures housing some two thousand monks and nuns. Most important, the urge to further conquest was postponed while Empress Feng encouraged the growth and development of government. She had aristocratic Chinese officials play a key role in crafting policies and institutions that significantly enhanced state power. These were the so-called Taihe Reforms of 472–492. They included procedures for evaluating and promoting regional and local officials; graded official salaries; a law code; an "equal field" system of land allotments; and a system of organizing households for taxation and control purposes based on multiples of five, each with a responsible leader. Not since the time of Cao Cao, 250 years earlier, or even then, had anything like this been done anywhere in China.

The Northern Wei did not survive the repercussions of its next big move, which was the abandonment of Pingcheng, and the rebuilding de novo of Luoyang far to the south in the heart of China proper. This was another totally planned capital city, a kind of Pingcheng, but on a grander scale. Recurrent food crises and a desire to be closer to the southern battlefronts seem to have contributed to this move, but perhaps the main motive was Emperor Xiaowen's desire to escape the tribal milieu of the far north and place his capital in a Chinese environment more hospitable to his autocratic impulses. Forced labor, and the forced relocation of many tens of thousands of people, again became the order of the day. So was compulsory social engineering. Emperor Xiaowen was determined to create stability at the center, and to that end, he envisioned a world of ranked, fixed, and hereditary social classes, all living in designated urban wards, or in the countryside under official control, with officialdom recruited strictly from among the prominent lineages. There was a Chinese aristocracy of lineages. There were neither lineages nor aristocracy among the Xianbi, and so by an edict of 495, Xiaowen created an aristocracy and commanded that it be integrated with the Chinese into a single pool. Ethnic intermarriage at the higher ranks was encouraged. At court, the Xianbi language, clothing, and tribal religion were forbidden. Surnames had to conform to Chinese usages. In line with that requirement, the ruling

Tuoba tribe changed its own name from Tuoba to Yuan. (The model for much of this was the aristocratic Western Jin.)

The move to Luoyang was fiercely opposed by many forced evacuees, but especially by the tribes left behind in the north. This problem was never remedied. The Northern Wei survived barely a quarter century in Luoyang before it collapsed in the frontier-wide Revolt of the Six Garrisons. Until the outbreak of that disaster, sheer central power achieved wondrous results. Under the direction of another dowager empress, this one née Hu (a Chinese aristocrat from Gansu), there were built in Luoyang over five hundred lavish Buddhist temples, a spectacular pagoda (the Yongning), and, not far from Luoyang, the stupendous cave statues of Buddhas at Longmen (somewhat replicating those carved earlier at Yungang). Royalty and high aristocracy enjoyed huge mansions, fantastic wealth, and native and imported luxuries of every kind. But not for long. After five years of frontier insurrections, on May 17, 528, the army of the Jie warlord and erstwhile Shanxi ranching chief Erzhu Rong marched on Luoyang, seized Dowager Empress Hu and the baby emperor, and drowned them in the Yellow River. His men slaughtered upward of a thousand officials and high elites. Yet again, the horrors of civil war and chaos blanketed north China. By 534, Luoyang was a total ruin. It would have been hard to guess then that the reunification of all China lay just a half century in the future, and that the force behind it would issue from the north.

Another China, meanwhile, lay south of the Huai river system. Nominally, it occupied a huge territory, reaching as far south as present-day Vietnam. In population and resources, however, it was heavily overshadowed by north China. The south was ruled by a succession of rather weak governments whose capitals were placed mainly at Jiankang, but also at times up the Yangzi River at Jiangling. The Eastern Jin (318–420) was the longest lasting of the southern regimes, although it was never able effectively to register and tax its population. It suffered under a succession of juvenile and dysfunctional emperors, as well as from factional struggles among the leading families. Many of its talented intellectuals and writers were disinclined to lend the regime their best efforts. Nevertheless, a series of military dictators managed to make the Eastern Jin a serious player in the all-China power game. In fact, there was more southern aggression against the north than northern aggression against the south. Dictator Huan Wen conquered Sichuan in 347. There were several short-lived recoveries of the old capital of Luoyang and of Chang'an as well. Dictator Liu Yu captured two northern rulers, brought them as prisoners to Jiankang, and there had them decapitated. And earlier, in 383, dictator Xie An foiled Fu Jian's attempt to conquer the south. But more usual than war were diplomacy, alliance making, and peaceful defections back and forth from one side to the other. The north never developed the riverborne forces necessary for the conquest of the south, while the south failed to organize the materiel and manpower needed for siege warfare in the north. Neither side had bureaucracies capable of permanently occupying and administering such territory as was temporarily seized from the other.

The southern warlords and military dictators predicated the legitimacy of the Eastern Jin upon its determination to recover the lost north. But for many, perhaps most, of the several million upper-class northern émigrés who took over southern society and its civil government, the legitimacy of the Jin and its successors lay not in reconquest but in its symbolic defense of China's literati culture (*wen*). The émigré poets, philosophers, critics, historians, and anthologists indeed far outnumbered and outweighed in importance their counterparts who stayed in the north. Whereas the literati disdained political ambition, a swollen roster of official positions served their need for status. They were a service aristocracy, their relative social ranking a vital concern that only a dynastic state could supervise for them. But the dynastic states they served—after the Eastern Jin came the Liu-Song, the (Southern) Qi, the (Southern) Liang, and the Chen—weakened as time went on.

Not by Blood Alone: Steps to Reunification 534–589

When the Northern Wei collapsed in frontier revolts, two regimes emerged: one in the east under Gao Huan (d. 547), a frontiersman of mixed Chinese and Xianbi heritage and a former follower of

Erzhu Rong; the other in the west (Guanzhong) under Yuwen Tai (d. 556), also a frontiersman, of Xianbi and Xiongnu descent, and also Erzhu Rong's former officer. Both men ruled behind Northern Wei puppet emperors. Gao's realm was the larger in population and resources, so when his son Gao Yang founded his own Northern Qi dynasty in 550, he had definite advantages over all rivals. But things went very badly. A Jie general—Hou Jing—defected with his entire army to the Southern Liang (where he was murdered in 552, after his failed attempt to set up his own dynasty at Jiankang). Far from easing ethnic tensions, Gao Yang exacerbated them by favoring Xianbi over Chinese. He suffered from progressive insanity, flew into murderous rages, and died in 559 at the age of 31. Northern Qi attacks on the troubled Southern Liang came to nothing.

In the west, meanwhile, Yuwen Tai and a collegium of Xianbi and Chinese generals ruling behind another puppet emperor fared rather better. They captured the cruel and violent Southern Liang emperor at Jiangling and executed him on January 25, 555. They accommodated a major defector, Xiao Cha, and his whole army by making him ruler of a Later Liang dynasty at Jiangling. Yuwen's generals returned to Chang'an with a large number of captives whom they enslaved. Their main enemy was, however, the Eastern Wei/Northern Qi. Yuwen deflected two major invasions of Guanzhong by Gao Huan in 537. In 538 and 543, Gao in turn defeated major thrusts eastward by Yuwen. Things then settled into a long stalemate. Gao held a distinct edge in cavalry and in overall numbers. Yuwen had to make do with a mixed fighting force of Di, Qiang, and Chinese, plus a small Xianbi cavalry, but his superior organizing overcame his disadvantages. Many details of his military reforms are unclear, but there was a heavy reliance on Chinese peasant recruits, who were well treated, given Xianbi surnames, and granted tax exemptions. Their commanders were Yuwen's associates, who had no personal ties to them, a feature that helped ensure the loyalty of everyone, commanders as well as troops, to the center. The small Western Wei regime grew with the conquest of Gansu in the 540s and Sichuan in 553.

The Western Wei ended with the murder of its puppet emperor and the founding of a new dynasty, the Northern Zhou, on February 15, 557. The nominal founding ruler was Yuwen Tai's very young son, whose cousin Yuwen Hu, a self-styled latter-day Duke of Zhou (semilegendary founder of the ancient Confucian political order), sponsored the reorganization of the new government along Confucian lines. Of this, the principal architect was a Chinese scholar-official, Su Chuo (498–546), a stern Confucianist whose program of personal and political morality, economic sufficiency, tax fairness, and careful official recruitment certainly helped guide the process of institutionalization that provided a major key to political stabilization and, eventually, the reunification of China.

The unhappy Northern Qi regime was severely weakened by a Chen attack from the south in 573, and it was finally destroyed by its archrival the Northern Zhou in 577. The leader who successfully pressed that assault despite strong advice to the contrary was Emperor Wu, who personally murdered regent Yuwen Hu in 572 and was—surprisingly, perhaps—the only effective sovereign the dynasty ever had. By 577, he controlled all of China except the Chen-held lower Yangzi. Emperor Wu intended to take it, but in 578 death cheated him of the opportunity.

Wu's son and successor died in 580. In 581, the dead successor's father-in-law, Yang Jian, a Chinese high official and general, having killed fifty-nine members of the Yuwen imperial family, deposed the last Northern Zhou emperor, a child, and founded his own Sui dynasty (581–618). In 588, six Sui armies attacked the Chen from the north while a navy sailed downstream from Sichuan (essentially, a repeat of the Western Jin strategy of 280). Early in 589 the Chen capital, Jiankang, was breached. The city was then completely razed and made into farmland. The Chen emperor and his court were transported to Chang'an. Some four centuries of disunion were over. China was reunified.

PART 2

Imperial Grandeur and Its Aftermath 589–907

Sui and early Tang China shared the Eurasian landmass with several other empires of great size: the Umayyad, the Byzantine, and, a little later, the Carolingian. Most featured glittering capital cities (Chang'an, Baghdad, and Constantinople), cultural and artistic brilliance, and dominating imperial personalities. All were overstretched, and all shrank over time. In China, the Sui and early Tang dynasties featured a top-heavy, centralized infrastructure of military, political, and fiscal institutions that had been pioneered in the later stages of the preceding age of disunion. These institutions, described in elaborate written statutes and directives, and staffed by trained bureaucrats, served the Sui and especially the Tang well for about a century and a half.

The suddenness with which the Sui reunified China in 589 and immediately went on to copy the early Han and create an extra-China empire, which is to say a zone of security surrounding China to the north and west, only to collapse in 618, reminds one of earlier short-lived unifying dynasties: the Qin (221–206 BCE), and of course the Western Jin (266–311). Whereas there are interesting parallels between the Qin and the Sui (as well as between the Former Han and the Tang), the Sui and Western Jin do not compare very well, and that is in some major respects a measure of the institutional and other changes that had taken place over the intervening centuries. The Sui rulers were in a position to bring about some spectacular accomplishments, which the Jin rulers were not, because, thanks to the panoply of earlier state-centered measures developed by the Northern Wei and the Northern Zhou, the Sui founder, Yang Jian, was in effective control of the economic and human resources of the entirety of a China whose population and production were on the rebound. The puzzling question, then, is why the Sui enjoyed so short a mandate (thirty-seven years). The answer surely has to be searched for in Sui leadership at the top: Given immense resources, what did the Sui emperors do with those resources, once reunification was achieved? The institutions of the time, by themselves, could not save a regime confused as to its goals and bent upon squandering its resources, immense as those may have been. The Tang founders resumed command of much the same set of centralizing institutions as the Sui had commanded, but used them to rather better effect, and the result was by many measures—cultural and artistic certainly, but also political, religious, military, and administrative—one of the high points in the whole history of imperial China.

The central machinery of early Tang government seems to have brought Northern Wei, Northern Zhou, and Sui precedents to something of a pinnacle of rationality and efficiency. The busy center of it all featured the emperor, with such palace organs and assistants as he (or she—the empress Wu) might choose. Outside the palace, the emperor personally supervised the academicians, the Censorate, and the three highest executive organs (handling policy formulation and recommendation; policy review and revision; and policy implementation, mainly through the Six Ministries—Personnel, Revenue, Rites, War, Justice, and Works). There were in addition many other bureaus. One of them was the Directorate of Education, which had charge of several central schools, including an upper-tier School for Sons of State (*guozi xue*), whose student body numbered some three hundred young men from the highest social and official classes, and a lower-tier National University (*taixue*) for some five hundred students of more modest pedigree. The expectation was that they would all one day be recruited into appropriate positions in bureaucracy.

There were a number of entryways for new recruits into early Tang bureaucracy, which was divided into nine ranks and grew in size from fourteen thousand in 657 to around nineteen thousand in 737. In 737, there were some 137 eligible sons of high officials, guardsmen, clerks, and capital and prefectural students competing for entry, and in any given year, about two thousand could be found vying for appointment to some five to six hundred vacancies. The most prestigious route of entry was by way of passing the competitive written examinations, of which there were originally several kinds, but clearly the most sought after was the *jinshi* degree, awarded for demonstrated literary talent. Examinations at first emphasized administrative competence, but in 736 the management of the system was shifted from the Ministry of Personnel to the Ministry of Rites (where it remained, until the abolition of the examination system in 1905). The shift was significant; mere administrative competence had become too commonplace a requirement, and the dynasty was persuaded to recognize and reward the rarer talents of the realm. The *jinshi* examination was held annually in the capital, where about 400 aspirants vied for some 20 to 30 degrees. But the Tang examination system, for all the attention lavished upon it then and later, had a rather modest effect upon government. Mainly, the system was a mechanism for giving merit awards to the wellborn and well educated. More than identifying a political elite, it identified an intellectual elite.

The good and glorious times of empire lasted for about a century and a half. It all ended with the horrific An Lushan rebellion of 755–763, after which the Tang was restored, although on a quite different institutional footing. Hindsight suggests that the Sui and early Tang were China's answer to a major and prolonged crisis—that is, to a set of problems dating as far back as the end of the Later Han. The Tang empire was the handiwork of several generations of statesmen, intellectuals, and rulers, and it succeeded in what it aimed to do: restore the dynastic state to a position of comprehensive predominance over every major aspect of existence (economic, social, religious, intellectual, military, etc.) in every part of the country. And from that position, indeed, the early Tang radiated influences well beyond China. Early Tang models also exerted influence long after the end of the Tang itself, thanks to the high quality of the early Tang compilation and codification of its legal, ritual, governmental, and other systems.

There were weak spots in the institutional tapestry, however. After the An Lushan rebellion, the rips and tears could no longer be patched or hidden away. The biggest problem was military. The key question, not solved until the Song founding in 960, was how to organize and manage what had become a very large military establishment, now that the central state had lost much of the control it had earlier exercised over its people and national resources.

During the two hundred years leading up to the Song, there were a series of attempts to settle the matter, and for students of institutional history, these centuries are of great interest, especially because other changes—cultural, intellectual, religious, and administrative—were involved as well. But it is time now for a closer look at this period of union, starting with the Sui.

Unification by the Short-lived Sui 581–618

The emperor-dominated Sui dynasty, commanding the resources of a newly unified realm, embarked on a gigantic program of internal construction and foreign aggression unparalleled since the heyday of the Qin in the third century BCE. Chang'an, Luoyang, and Jiankang, wrecked in war or razed, were rebuilt as completely new cities on new foundations. The Grand Canal was dug at great speed, using massive hordes of conscript laborers, to link the rice of the lower Yangzi (Jiangnan) with Luoyang to the northwest and, from there, northeast to northern Hebei. A "great wall" was built, or rebuilt, using the fortifications already put in place by the Northern Qi and the Northern Zhou regimes.

The Sui founder, Yang Jian (Wendi, r. 581–604) exhibited a furious energy. He also sought some kind of superordinate doctrine for a dynasty that, for all its power, did not command much love or loyalty on its own merits. He gave an early nod to the Daoist church. For a while he favored a national system of Confucian schools; then, disappointed in the results, he abolished it in 601. Finally, he turned to Buddhism, specifically southern China's Tiantai sect, as a source of Sui legitimacy. Wendi became Buddhism's great defender and foremost patron. His model was nothing Chinese, but India's King Aśoka. At the practical end of things, as Su Chuo served the Northern Zhou, so Gao Jiong (555–607) served the Sui—as strategist and chief architect of its social, legal, and fiscal systems. In this Su Chuo's son, Su Wei (540–621), gave him important help. The national census of the early seventh century showed a healthy 8.9 million households, 46 million individuals, still heavily concentrated in the north.

The Sui regime, though not wholly sure of itself, was institutionally well grounded and should have lasted for centuries, as did its successor, the Tang. However, the Sui fell apart during the reign of just its second emperor, Yangdi (r. 604–618). Traditional history, with some justice, places the blame on him personally. Yangdi was a headstrong autocrat in sole command of an autocratic system. He became obsessed with the misbehavior and defiance of the small Korean state of Koguryŏ, which sat astride the Yalu River and, as Yangdi saw it, threatened the security of northeastern China through its alliance with a new power in the northern steppes, the Tujue (Turks). There was an unstable situation in the China-Korea-Manchuria triangle, to be sure. Wendi had made careful plans to invade Koguryŏ in 598, but after he lost 80 percent of his three hundred thousand men to storms, flood, famine, and disease, he was forced to cancel the attack. Yangdi resumed the offensive four times by land and sea. He led in person some six hundred thousand men in 612. There were further thrusts in 613, 614, and finally 615. Logistical breakdowns, food shortages, and massive desertions forced each expedition to a halt. Yangdi's relentless determination—or madness—eventually turned his own class of people, the Sino-barbarian elite of northwest China, against him in rebellion. His own military commanders strangled him in his headquarters in south China in 618. That ended the Sui.

The Long-lived Tang
618–907

Between the outbreak of the first anti-Sui rebellions in 612 and the Tang destruction of its last major rival in 621, there elapsed but nine years of chaos and war. Why was this period of disunion so short, as compared to the situation from the third to the sixth centuries? There is no easy answer. At the outset, the splintering of military power was extreme, with hundreds of independent roving bandit gangs, local self-defense forces, and autonomous local officials. By 618, strong leaders had consolidated all these into nine empire-seeking warlord organizations. Then, in what has been styled a "bandwagon effect," it turned out that the armies led by Li Yuan and his intrepid younger son Li Shimin held the clear upper hand in leadership quality, overall strategy, and battlefield tactics. There was no die-hard resistance to them. In 621, it was all over.

Of course, the rise of the Latter Zhao and the Former Qin earlier on could also be described as rapid. What was different about the Tang was its adoption and further development of all the institutional groundwork laid earlier. That, and the happy circumstance that five of its first seven rulers were capable, and of them, two (Li Shimin and Empress Wu) were exceptionally capable. Tang power and its durability owe much to geopolitical context, domestic institutions, and the accident of effective leadership.

Until the Communist Revolution of 1949, no state exercised so direct a control over the agrarian and commercial life of China as did the early Tang. It micromanaged much of north China landholding through its "equal field" system, first instituted in the Northern Wei, which aimed to assign abandoned farmland on an equal basis to cultivators and their families; to periodically redistribute the land as families grew larger or smaller; to extract equal amounts of grain, cloth, and labor services from each unit of land; to prevent the rise of a private landlord class (the central state was sole landlord); and to ensure the state a steady income. The great damage the Sui-Tang civil wars had inflicted upon north China made idle land plentiful and labor scarce, thus making state management of national agriculture feasible. (Still, it took decades for the Tang to reestablish the same degree of control over the realm that the Sui had imposed.) Running this system required a veritable army of clerks and accountants, and tons of paper reports, some remains of which have been recovered in the desert climate of Dunhuang and Turfan in Xinjiang. Central offices maintained constant surveillance over local officials in the carrying out of this system (monasteries, high officials, and probably all of south China lay outside the equal fields domain). In addition, Tang officials directly operated nearly a thousand state farms along the western and northern frontiers to supply some six hundred thousand garrison soldiers.

The Tang government also controlled nearly all dimensions of trade: local, interregional, international. Merchants were officially discriminated against, and most private trade was either discouraged or forbidden. Local officials ran local markets, setting prices and conditions of sale. The central government monopolized interregional trade, itself transporting huge quantities of grain and cloth over the Grand Canal every year from south China to Luoyang and Chang'an. A maritime trade office at Canton dominated foreign commerce there, while state-run frontier markets monopolized cloth-for-horses transactions, mainly with the Tujue Turks.

The main Tang capital was the gigantic planned city of Chang'an, begun by the Sui and completed early in the Tang. Though artificial and located at the edge of a reunified China, it became the world's largest city with a population of about one million. There were many foreign residents living in their separate wards in Chang'an, and the city enjoyed trade connections with Tibet, India, and the greater Middle East. However, the city's main function was as the center of government. The dominant people included the very large imperial establishment in its own palace quarter, some two thousand ranked central officials, plus larger numbers of clerks, soldiers, police, and students.

The Tang government managed not only the nation's agriculture and commerce, but social, religious, and intellectual life as well. As Wudi, emperor of the Southern Liang (r. 502–549), had done, so too the early Tang authorized, compiled, and published in 638 and again in 659 a national register of elite lineages whose members were certified as socially qualified for office. The 638 register recognized 1,651 lineages (sorted into nine grades), and the 659 register 2,287 (recognition more liberally granted on the basis of recent official service). This Tang "aristocracy" lacked legal privileges other than those granted actual holders of office, however.

Chang'an was the center of the Buddhist church, although most early Tang rulers did not embrace Buddhism as fervently as had the Sui rulers, or Liang Wudi, or indeed Shi Le or Fu Jian. The Tang founder's Li lineage claimed descent from Laozi, which made the imperial house rather more favorable toward the Daoist church than the Buddhist. Nevertheless, the Tang state closely supervised the Buddhist religious establishment and patronized learned sects such as the Tiantai and the Faxiang. When the monk Xuanzang, founder of the Faxiang sect, returned from India in 645, for example, Li Shimin funded his enormous plan to translate 1,347 Sanskrit holy texts. Secular or Confucian learning was also overwhelmingly concentrated in Chang'an under imperial support and patronage. Informal groups, advisory colleges, and bureaucratic scholarly agencies turned out a ritual code; a standard version of the Five Classics; dynastic histories of the post-Han age of disunion (in which Li was much interested personally; he even wrote some portions); and much else. The early Tang rulers made no effort to identify and enforce an orthodoxy, however, and open debate over scholarly issues was not discouraged.

In the city of Chang'an, in China, and indeed in greater East Asia as a whole, the one dominating figure was Emperor Li Shimin, known posthumously as Taizong. In 626 he killed two of his brothers, forced his imperial father into retirement, and seized direct rule for himself. The Li family were members of the same Sino-Xianbi aristocracy that had produced the founders of the Northern Zhou and Sui dynasties (Taizong's paternal grandmother was a Xianbi; his mother was a niece of Emperor Wu of the Northern Zhou). The ethos of that aristocracy featured hunting and war; to it Taizong, who was highly literate, added an intellectual bent. For the first dozen years of his reign, he was accessible and collegial, in contrast to the remote despotism practiced by the failed Sui Yangdi. After 636 or so, and down to the end of his life in 649, Taizong became autocratic, often sidestepping the regular administrative organs in favor of special operations of his own. Taizong's son and successor Gaozong (r. 649–683) was troubled by lifelong health problems, but his consort, Empress Wu (d. 705), proved extremely capable. She disfavored Chang'an and ruled mostly from Luoyang, which was rebuilt yet again, and at great expense. Chang'an, and Tang China, reached their apogee of power, prestige, and cultural brilliance under Xuanzong (r. 712–756). A long succession of effective rulers, plus strong institutional support, explain the early Tang success and the high visibility of the Tang in the world of its time and in history to this day.

The Tang as Empire

The early Tang rulers, being history minded, looked back to the Former Han as a yardstick for their own endeavors in empire building beyond China. The Former Han, however, had waited several generations after its founding in 206 BCE before it began pursuing empire. Tang empire building began almost immediately.

Power in the steppes was held by the Eastern Turks, or Tujue. To win their temporary military support, the Tang founder, Li Yuan (later called Taizu), had gone so far as to accept their suzerainty. But his son, Taizong, personally confronted the Tujue and in 630 inflicted a heavy defeat upon them. Large numbers of surrendered Turks were made to settle inside China and in Chang'an as a military reserve. In an impressive ceremony held that same year, Taizong assumed an additional title—Celestial Khaghan. (This had a precedent of sorts in the preceding era, when several non-Chinese rulers bore simultaneously the titles "emperor" for the Chinese and *shanyu* for the Inner Asians). There followed the destruction of the Tuyuhun in Qinghai in 634; the conquest of the Xinjiang oases in the 630s and 640s; and three land-and-sea attacks on Koguryŏ (644–649). As in the case of the bigger but failed Sui campaigns earlier, the strategic reasons for the Tang assaults on Koguryŏ are not entirely clear. Likewise, despite one great tactical victory, Taizong's campaigns in Korea ultimately failed. Taizong's justification for his expansionism was ethical: to spread righteousness and crush disorder worldwide.

Although large gains were no longer to be had, the Tang successfully defended its empire for a century after Taizong's death. Imperial expansion had been achieved using small numbers of highly trained offensive fighting forces plus Turk auxiliaries. But defending the empire was different: defense demanded large armies placed in permanent garrisons along the frontiers. Permanent frontier garrisons had ended Northern Wei rule in 534, and, in due course, they would vex Tang China as well. Other institutional changes were afoot, including especially the partial breakdown of the equal field system. State-managed land allotments became a victim of their own success, as land available for redistribution in north China became scarce, and people in great numbers migrated south, beyond the system's reach. Heroic efforts were made to save the system, particularly in 723 and 724 by Yuwen Rong. (The system collapsed completely in the wake of the An Lushan rebellion of 755–763).

Over the long term, the greater geopolitical environment more and more disfavored the Tang empire. In the seventh century, except for Koguryŏ, only loosely organized tribal entities such as the Tujue and Tuyuhun ringed China. In the eighth century, the Tang faced formidably organized states in the newly risen empires of Tibet and Nanzhao. The Tibetan threat was so serious, and so close to Chang'an, that in 676 the Tang evacuated Korea and south Manchuria for good in order to face it. A complex infrastructure of forts, garrisons, and military farms was built up along the Tibetan frontier. Then, during the years 736 to 752, under the direction of the aristocrat Li Linfu, a new system of permanent frontier defense commands was set up, stretching from the northeast all the way out into Xinjiang in the west. In 749, Li abolished the last remnant of the inherited self-supporting militia system that had won Tang the empire. It was now obsolete. Because the commanders of the new permanent garrisons would necessarily be powerful figures with personal ties to their troops, Li persuaded Xuanzong in 748 to order that those commanders should be ethnically non-Chinese since they made better fighters and lacked potentially dangerous connections in high government circles. The result of this ill-advised policy change was almost immediately catastrophic. The central government did not closely supervise the new appointees. In 755, the commander of several northeastern garrisons, a general of mixed Sogdian and Turkish descent named An Lushan, rebelled with his army and declared a new dynasty. For eight years, war raged across north China. Xuanzong fled Chang'an. A new Tang ruler, Suzong, supported by loyalist military governors, defectors from rebel ranks, and four thousand Uighur horsemen, finally destroyed the last of the rebels in 763. Chang'an was damaged. Luoyang was plundered and burned. Peace was restored, but autonomous military governors, especially in An's old bailiwick in the northeast (present-day Hebei), remained as a problem not settled until the founding of the Song dynasty two centuries in the future.

After Empire: Reconstructing China

When the dust cleared after the An Lushan rebellion, Tang China was a smaller and a much-changed place. It was no longer an empire. Xinjiang, Gansu, and Qinghai fell to Tibet. The Uighurs, who followed the Tujue in dominating the northern steppes, placed Tang China under their military protection and profited greatly from the exchange of their horses for Tang silk. Tibet allied itself with Nanzhao and looked culturally to India rather than China. The Uighurs accepted the Manichean religion of their Sogdian merchant trading partners. Korea and south Manchuria came under the strong states of Silla and Parhae, respectively, and were no longer targets of Tang aggression.

But as in the earlier case of the Later Han, so the Tang after its loss of empire experienced a very likely increase in overall domestic prosperity. The years after An Lushan saw profound changes in the way China was administered. No longer did the central government manage society directly. Instead, it did so indirectly. Some forty new territorial units called provinces came to be placed between the central government and the many preexisting smaller units, the prefectures and counties. Among the rural population there emerged a new class of private landlords. From 780, instead of the old equal field assessments, a new imposition called the twice-a-year tax was laid on property, not people. Amounts were determined by negotiation—between the provinces and lower units, and between the center and the provinces. In south China from 760, a different fiscal apparatus prevailed, imposed by a special commission sent by the central government to Yangzhou on the Grand Canal, where it seized control of salt production, sold the salt to private merchants at very high prices, and used the proceeds to fund tax shipments and to pay directly into the imperial coffers. In both north and south, government control receded, and private landlords and merchants advanced. National productivity began an upward leap (as it did after the abandonment of collective farming in 1976).

The Tang central government, despite its reduced role, was still active after 763. The throne became for a while a rallying point for an emerging Confucian intelligentsia that was taking advantage of the competitive civil service examination system both to make of itself a meritocracy and, as such, to champion political reform. Several of the later Tang emperors strove to reduce the autonomy of the provincial military governors and recentralize the realm. Dezong (d. 805) tried to use military force to eliminate the Hebei governors, but supply problems and a mutiny ended the attempt. An examination degree-holder, the southerner Lu Zhi successfully steered Dezong through the crisis and gained undying fame in so doing. Dezong's sickly son and successor reigned scarcely a year. Palace eunuchs then enthroned Xianzong (r. 805–820), who enjoyed more success. He recentralized all but Hebei and placed all the central military forces under the supervision of the palace eunuchs; but his reign ended on a sour note, as he suffered from elixir poisoning in an attempt to achieve immortality and became less able to govern.

Eunuch power emerged after the An Lushan rebellion and was in part a consequence of it. Recruited largely from among non-Chinese aborigines of the extreme south, the eunuchs were castrated as children and came to be schooled in the palace and appointed military supervisors, or commanders of the Shence ("Divine Strategy") Army. This army was originally organized to fight An Lushan, and it was subsequently centralized, well fed, well trained, and freed of all legal restraints. By 820, there were 4,018 palace eunuchs.

The eunuchs had enemies. In 805, a cabal of inner court officials tried but failed to overpower them. In 835, a violent attempt by the officials to remove the eunuchs ended in a horrific bloodbath, as the eunuchs retaliated in fury and massacred some three thousand officials in Chang'an and elsewhere. That decisively ended all lingering hope that the Tang government could be reformed at the center by the direct action of scholar-officials.

Confucianism and Buddhism in the Late Tang

In the century following the An Lushan rebellion, a handful of literati, graduates of the examination system, pioneered a revival of Confucianism. The leading figures were Han Yu (768–819), Li Ao (774–836), and Liu Zongyuan (773–819). Early in the Tang, the Confucians had been court-centered officials, patronized by rulers. The new breed were no longer court centered and were no longer content with the tepid and circumscribed Confucianism of earlier times. Liu conceded religious truth to Buddhism but aimed to reestablish the primacy of Confucianism as political philosophy. Li and Han, more ambitious, aimed also to recapture and reassert the inner core of Confucianism as a supreme guide to ethical self-renewal. All three, but especially Han, were devotees of what was called "ancient prose" (guwen), an expressive and refreshing change from the by-now stale standards set in south China in the centuries preceding the Sui unification and still required in the Tang examinations.

Despite their great celebrity, the late Tang Confucian revivalists did not dominate the world of their time, at least not politically, save for occasional spectacular political protests. As noted earlier, most positions were assigned not to the successful examinations takers, but to guardsmen, senior clerks, and the sons of high officials. Corruption was rife and occasionally spectacular. Weak emperors, who often died young of elixir poisoning, let power gravitate into the hands of finance experts, eunuchs, or Daoist holy men. In the provinces, many of them autonomous or semiautonomous, Chan Buddhism prevailed, as the Chan patriarchs came to merge Buddhism with the Chinese family order and Confucian ritual.[1]

Authorities in the separatist provinces were able to offer some protection to the Buddhists in the furious throne-directed destruction of Buddhism in the years 845 and 846. Led into this wreckage by Daoist pleadings, by envy of the church's wealth, and by the long-standing complaint that Buddhism was a foreign religion, the emperor Wuzong (r. 840–846) was soon able to boast of closing over 4,600 monasteries, confiscating enormous tracts of church land, laicizing two hundred sixty thousand monks and nuns, and reselling or redistributing one hundred fifty thousand church slaves. All foreign monks were deported from China. All other foreign religions were closed down as well: Nestorian churches, Zoroastrian temples, and—thanks to the collapse of the sponsoring Uighur khanate—Manichean temples, whose scriptures were burned and whose priests were executed. Shortly after Wuzong's death in 846, the bans were lifted, but irreparable damage had been done.

In 840, during the reign of this same Wuzong, the steppe-based Uighur empire had collapsed, sending large numbers of refugees together with their leaders west into Xinjiang and southeast to the Tang frontier, where they asked the Tang court for refuge. The Tang, by now a weak and insecure state, feeling threatened by the Nanzhao kingdom in the south and Tibet just to the west, hoped to persuade the

---

1. "Chan" is sometimes given its Japanese pronounciation, "Zen."

Uighurs to leave the border region and return home. But negotiations proved unavailing, and so in February 843, the Tang, using a force of Tuyuhun, Shatuo Turks, and other allies, attacked the Uighurs' main camp and massacred them. All Uighurs living in China were ordered to wear Chinese-style clothing. Uighur shops and houses were confiscated, along with the Manichean temples. No power dominated the northern steppes again until the rise of Chinggis Khan's Mongols in the early 1200s.

The Shattering of the Tang 868–907

An increasingly destructive series of internal revolts that began in the south in 868 brought about the end of the Tang in 907. The problem mainly stemmed from the increasing militarization of interior China after the An Lushan rebellion of 755–763. In An Lushan's time, six hundred thousand troops were posted on the frontiers. A half century later, nearly twice that number occupied the northern provinces, mainly in the interior. No longer the serflike dependents of commanders as in the third and fourth centuries, the soldiers of the late Tang were volunteers, free agents given to mutiny when their rewards and bonuses were delayed or cancelled. The Pang Xun mutiny of 868 broke out among Henan troops and their officers sent far to the southwest to fight the Nanzhao kingdom. Unchecked, the rebels marched back north to Henan, adding peasants and bandits to their numbers as they went. The Tang had to call upon four thousand Shatuo Turk horsemen to suppress this affair in 869.

The infamous Huang Chao rebellion of 875–884 was not a military mutiny, however. It began as a consolidation of gangs in the famine-wracked area of present-day Henan and Shandong. Huang Chao, who rose to lead this force, was a civilian, one of many thousands who unsuccessfully took the civil service examination. Like a swarm of locusts, the rebels went on a murderous long march through weakly defended south China to Canton, then back north to Luoyang and Chang'an, which they occupied in 881. The eunuch-led Shence Army had by this time become corrupt and useless, and the emperor

Xizong and his court fled south to Sichuan. In Chang'an, Huang announced a new dynasty and held civil service examinations to recruit officials for it; but his army, lacking a tax base or source of supply, turned to plunder and massacre, while elsewhere in north China the military governors reconsidered the allegiance they had earlier pledged to him. The Tang court obtained the help of Shatuo Turk leader Li Keyong and his cavalry and secured the defection from Huang's forces of the commander Zhu Wen and his army. Together, Li and Zhu drove off Huang Chao, who committed suicide, or was killed, in the summer of 884. Xizong retuned to Chang'an. Remnants of Huang's armies continued the rebellion until 889.

Institutional decline reached a nadir in the late ninth century. Nominally, the Tang still ruled, but it was at the mercy of Li and Zhu, who fought each other for control of the court. Autonomous military governors ruled much of north China. In Sichuan, a former bandit by the name of Wang Jian set up an independent regime with the aid of former Tang officials including the Daoist scholar Du Guangting and the litterateur Wei Zhuang. Elsewhere in the south, former rebels against and local defenders of the empire took power: in Fujian, it was the outlaw Wang brothers from Henan; in Zhejiang, a salt smuggler and local defender named Qian Liu. In north China, Huang's former follower Zhu (originally from a family of classics teachers that had fallen on hard times) applied the coup de grâce to the Tang. He murdered the last Tang emperor, massacred the eunuchs, and abandoned Chang'an to establish his own regime (the first of the so-called Five Dynasties of north China) at a new location—Bianzhou (Kaifeng) in Henan. Thus began the era of the Five Dynasties and Ten Kingdoms (907–960).

In fact, political breakdown affected not just China at this time, but all of greater East Asia as well. The Uighur khanate collapsed in 840, as noted previously. The once-powerful Tibetan empire fell apart in the 840s and 850s, never to return. The state of Nanzhao in what is now Yunnan province broke up after 902. Annam slipped out of China's control and from 939 became independent. In the northeast, the state of Parhae (its rulers of Koguryŏ stock imposing a Tang-style administration over the subject Malgal people) disappeared in 926. On the Korean peninsula, a unified realm, Silla, broke into three warring parts after 889.

The Five Dynasties and Ten Kingdoms 907–960

The Five Dynasties era is poorly served by source material and is still understudied, and it is not clear how China's inherited unifying values and systems managed to survive all the stress and turmoil. There is no obvious answer to the question of just what is (or was) "China," or to what extent after a breakdown it "naturally" comes together as one unified and coherent civilization. It helps, however, to compare the late Tang and Five Dynasties period of 907 to 960 with the early medieval scene of 221 to 589.

The south China regional governments of the Ten Kingdoms period were rivals, yet they were less bent on war than were the Southern Dynasties of 221 to 589, preferring to use diplomacy in an intricate game of power balancing. The richest, longest lasting, and perhaps strongest of the southern group was the Wu-Yue state founded by Qian Liu in Zhejiang province, which lasted from 907 to 978. Uninterested in achieving national power, the Wu-Yue rulers were content to acknowledge the overlordship of the militarized northern regimes, which accorded Wu-Yue a status just short of imperial. In return, Wu-Yue funneled lavish tribute to, and facilitated economic relations with, the resource-starved north. On its own, Wu-Yue conducted diplomatic and trade relations with the Khitans of the northeast, the three Korean states, and Japan. But Wu-Yue's western neighbor, the Southern Tang, had even closer relations with the Khitans, hoping thereby to counterbalance Wu-Yue's ties with various dynasties of north China.

The Canton-based Southern Han regime, meanwhile, carried on a very large trade with Indonesia, as a recent discovery of a shipwreck makes clear. The ship was Southeast Asian and when it sank it was carrying Chinese silver ingots, lead coins, ceramics, and other commodities now difficult to identify.

Within months of Zhu Wen's deposition of the last Tang emperor in June 907, Wang Jian down in Sichuan declared himself emperor of a fully independent Great Shu dynasty, with its capital in Chengdu. He welcomed literati fleeing the disorders in the north and initiated a major cultural program involving the construction of palaces, bridges, and pleasure parks, the inauguration of musical ensembles, the encouragement of painting, and the sponsorship and publication of a new poetic form, the song-lyric (*ci*). Conquered and annexed by the Latter Tang (one of the Five Dynasties) in 926, the Great Shu regime rose again when its provincial governor, Meng Zhixiang, declared his independence in 934. The earlier cultural program was revived, and the dynasty flourished until it was conquered yet again, this time by the Northern Song, in 965.

The rulers of the Southern Tang, who laid a legitimist claim to kinship with the imperial Li family, presented much the same profile as the Great Shu. Based in Nanjing, the Southern Tang court also patronized artists and literati, but its administrative efficiency and military power fell to neglect, and it was invaded and annexed by the Northern Song in 975. Had the Ten Kingdoms shown a better ability to entrench and defend themselves, China might have undertaken a devolved pattern of multistate development, culturally vibrant, and much different from the long-term drive toward uniformity and centralization that in fact took place.

In early medieval times, south China was not divided as it was in the tenth century, but politically united for the most part, and its dictators harbored desires to conquer the north, which was often in a state of political fragmentation. South China was commercially more active than the north, but the north held the great preponderance of population and resources. Centuries later, in the Ten Kingdoms era, many regional governments divided up south China. All of them fearfully expected an eventual takeover by one of the northern powers. In the earlier era, south China witnessed social conflicts among northern émigrés, a southern Chinese population established earlier, and a large presence of non-Chinese aborigines. Conflicts also divided Chinese aristocratic lineages from plebeian "cold gates" (families of obscure social origin). Then, assimilation quietly did its work. Centuries later, all these differences seem to have disappeared. Built up by steady immigration during the Tang era, south China's population grew to equal that of the north, and its resources became many times greater. Paradoxically, perhaps, a bigger and richer south China did not at this time translate its new advantages into political and military power.

PART 3

The Tripartition of China 960–1279

One is always tempted to attach the label "Song dynasty" to the period from 960 to 1279. The sheer size and cultural weight of the Northern Song (and later the Southern Song) indeed lend it importance of the first magnitude. With a landscape the size of modern France six times over, and as many as one hundred million people in its eleventh-century heyday, Northern Song China was unquestionably the largest and richest organized society on the face of the earth at the time. But it must not be forgotten (the Song rulers certainly did not forget) that there were two other "Chinas." The Xi Xia in the northwest may have numbered as many as three million people, half of them Han Chinese, the rest Tangut, Tibetan, Qiang, or Uighur. The Liao population, hard to estimate, must have been several times larger, with a dense Han Chinese population in the sixteen prefectures it acquired in China during the Five Dynasties era (most of Liao territory lay in Mongolia and Manchuria). (In the twelfth century, the Jin destroyed the Liao and conquered all of north China and a Chinese population of some forty million.) A constant source of irritation for the Song government was its inability to destroy those competitors and gather all the Sinophone peoples under one roof as in the Han and the Tang. The Northern Song, in order to enhance its military power, undertook some extraordinarily comprehensive efforts at institutional reform. But the irony is that the Song labored in vain. Its creativity meant it owed little to Han or Tang institutional precedents (Song reformers preferred to bypass the Han and Tang and engage with the remote Golden Age of Antiquity), and it left little in the way of a concrete institutional legacy for the future. The Liao and Jin had deep institutional roots in the Tang, and it was Liao, Jin, and Xi Xia institutions, not those of the Song, that influenced the deus ex machina that did reunify China: the Mongol Yuan dynasty of the thirteenth century.

The big problem that was never solved in the late Tang was regional military autonomy. With the removal of the Tang from the scene in 907, it was regional military rulers themselves in north China who, free to found dynasties of their own, worked out the institutional mechanisms that effectively brought the military back under central control. The Song dynasty, founded by way of a military coup in north China in 960, was an important contributor to, as well as beneficiary of, this process.

Then, a new set of problems emerged. With the conquest of south China, the Song came to rule a population that had approximately doubled between the sixth and the eleventh centuries, from fifty to as many as a hundred million. The per-acre productivity of China's agriculture had expanded as well, indeed creating a large surplus beyond subsistence that could flow into trade and taxation. There were so many people and so large a resource base that it made no sense to try to restore the micromanagerial apparatus of the Sui and early Tang—state control and periodic repartition of farmland, the state-run commercial economy, and so on. So, during the first century of Northern Song rule, its government, about the same size as that of the early Tang, could create in its part of "China" (by far the largest part) a general climate conducive to prosperity and further economic growth, while requiring but a modest tax income to support its work.

After a century of rule, however, it had become clear to many at court and among some of the educated elite that the Song was, in some essential respects, a failed state. Despite its size and wealth, it was militarily weak. Its inability to overpower the Xi Xia and the Liao put its legitimacy as a dynasty in question. What to do about this problem prompted an intense and ever-shifting partisan struggle that continued right down to the end of the Song altogether in 1279. But for three centuries, the power situation in East Asia avoided both the ruinous fragmentation of the post-Han era, as well as the often-stifling constraints of empire, and resembled closest the competitive multistate arrangement of Western Europe.

Song China has long had a rather misleading reputation as a wholly civilian, antimilitarist society, devoted to the Confucian classics and the peaceful arts overall. This picture has some truth to it, and the generally poor record of the Song in its wars with the Liao, Jin, and Xi Xia certainly reinforces it. However, it is well to remember that the Song founders were military men; that it was through warfare that most of China proper was physically reunited by 979; and that the professional Song army of some half-million soldiers became by far the largest armed force on the face of the globe in the eleventh century. It is also well to note that, especially in the north of Song-held China proper, there survived a long-standing tradition among the peasantry and some landowners of violence, martial arts, and a love of the military life. Marriage ties between the Song imperial house and the daughters of military officers was sustained throughout the Northern Song. It was also Song Chinese who pioneered the development of bombards and firearms. And irredentism—the hope of recapturing lost territory—was always a compelling issue in both the Northern and Southern Song. What the early Northern Song rulers did was not so much civilianize China so as to render it militarily weak; rather, in order to break the cycle of coups, they fragmented the military institutionally, using spies, hostages, and imperial directives to divide the command structure against itself and frequently transferring officers to discourage the growth of loyalties between commanders and troops. Whereas it is likely that these measures dampened Northern Song military effectiveness, bad strategic decisions on the part of top leadership were more to blame for Song defeats, and it is a fact that no coup or attempted coup by the military ever troubled the Song.

It is time now for a closer look at the long era of tripartition.

The Liao (927–1125), Northern Song (960–1126), and Xi Xia (982–1227)

The Five Dynasties of north China followed one after another, in a long spate of violence and turmoil, from 907 until the Song founding in 960. Through this violence there was gradually forged a political-military system of a new type that put an end to the provincial autonomy that, in mild or severe form, characterized China, the northeast especially, ever since the An Lushan rebellion of 755–763.

In essence, what happened was that as one provincial military governor's personal army and administrative machine kept expanding at the expense of his rivals', it became the nucleus of a wholly centralized new order, crystallized in the Song founding of 960.

That development, though important, does not paint the whole picture. If there were any paramount power in the fractured world of tenth-century East Asia, then it was none of the Five Dynasties of north China, but the confederation led by the Khitan (Qidan) people of Manchuria, whose leader, Yelü Deguang, announced the founding of the Liao dynasty in 927. This confederacy, in which the Khitans were an ethnic minority, was highly complex institutionally, with no exact parallel in the past. It controlled several different non-Khitan tribes in the steppes as far west as the Altai, as well as the former subjects of the Parhae state, Malgals or Jurchens for the most part, in south Manchuria. The Liao raided China on many occasions, bringing north captives whom it settled in some forty walled "Chinatowns" (*Hancheng*). Gradually, there evolved parallel systems of rule: one Liao government, mainly military, that ruled the tribal populations of Inner Asia and another Liao government, principally civilian, that replicated much of the old Tang order and ruled the settled Chinese population.

The chiefs of this confederacy—beginning with Yelü Abaoji (872–929) and continuing to his son Deguang (902–947), Deguang's nephew Yuan (918–951), and son Jing (931–969)—were caught in a cultural dilemma: How far to lean toward the Chinese model, how far to retain steppe traditions? The chiefs chose to intermarry exclusively with the Xiao clan of Uighur Turkish origin. They chose not to settle in any of the several capital cities they built, but rather to keep on the move, nomad style, in an elaborate tent complex. Abaoji tried, unsuccessfully, to end the consultative tribal system of governance and replace it with the patrilineal dynastic system of China. But many Khitans considered his son and designated heir Bei as too culturally Chinese and not enough of a fighting leader, and so his mother and other Khitan dignitaries denied him the succession. (Eventually, Bei fled to China, where he was murdered in 937).

The Liao, despite its difficult bipartite structure, was strong enough to meddle for years in the unsettled power situation on its southern frontier in China. This meddling reached an apex in the period from 936 to 938, when Shi Jingtang, the Shatuo Turk founder of the Latter

Jin dynasty, handed over sixteen frontier prefectures to the Liao in exchange for Liao aid in his overthrow of the Latter Tang. A few years later, however, Shi's successor repudiated the Liao. A four-year war followed, and in 947 the Liao army, led by the ruler Yelü Deguang, triumphantly occupied the Latter Jin capital at Kaifeng. But after five months' occupation, the Liao had to evacuate north China altogether, never to try to occupy it again as long as the dynasty lasted (to 1125). The Liao forces were harassed by armed resistance, and lacked the personnel, resources, and carefully drawn strategy to bring about a permanent occupation of all of north China. The sixteen prefectures were as much of "China" as they cared to try to control.

The Northern Song founder, a general by the name of Zhao Kuangyin, conducted what turned out to be the last successful military coup in China's dynastic history when he extinguished the Latter Zhou in Kaifeng in 960. With that act, all autonomous military governorships and commands were at last extinguished. From 960 to 979, the Song postponed a confrontation with the Liao over the sixteen prefectures, while it conducted an intensive series of diplomatic and military offensives to bring about the annexation of nearly all the rest of China.

The founding of the Khitan Liao state in the northeast preceded in date the Song in the center and south, and the Song preceded the founding of yet a third principal East Asian power, the Tangut Xi Xia state (982–1227) in the northwest. Like the Liao, the Xi Xia dynasty and state were Chinese in general format, but polyethnic in composition. The Xi Xia, however, did not adopt the Liao system of two governments. Founded by Li Jiqian, the Xi Xia expanded to include northern Shaanxi, Ningxia, and the Gansu corridor, at the west end of which it adjoined Uighur territory. Thus, whereas the extreme fragmentation of the Five Dynasties and Ten Kingdoms era was largely resolved by the late tenth century, the net result was no new unitary Han or Tang, but rather a three-way division of East Asia, with large Chinese populations inhabiting not just the Song, but Liao and Xi Xia territory as well. Institutionally, the Northern Song dynasty constitutes a peculiar phase in China's history, without either a distinct ancestry or a compelling institutional legacy for the future. In the eyes of many of its inhabitants, it should not have fallen so short of the Han and Tang standard. For all its wealth and power, the Song did not control an empire, did not govern all of East Asia's Chinese-speaking populations, and, at the outset, even within its own boundaries, did not reach effectively into society at large.

The three East Asian powers of the tenth to twelfth centuries were each compact, stable, and well organized as they faced each other in a kind of prolonged stalemate. Intermittent war between the Song and Liao over control of the Chinese-inhabited sixteen prefectures ended with the famous Treaty of Shanyuan of 1004, one term of which stipulated that the Song court would provide generous annual subsidies in silver and silk to the Liao court. Despite controversy, peace on the frontier prevailed for nearly a century thereafter. The Song disdained the Xi Xia and refused to accord it equal treatment with the Liao.

The great wealth and stability of Northern Song society has been attributed to the managerial expertise of its founding generations of high officials, men from sixty families from all parts of China who made their homes in Kaifeng, the capital, and who constituted an intermarried hereditary elite, quite similar to the mid-Tang aristocracy. But these men from privileged families were subjected to the rigors of an official examination system designed to identify early on men with legal, financial, and other special talents and direct them into the appropriate career channels. A friendly and predictable national climate for economic growth was the result. Moderate tax rates, a huge and gradually increasing supply of copper currency, safe conditions for interregional and international maritime trade, and government encouragement of and investment in industry (coal mining and iron production especially)—policies based upon administrative ideas first developed in the fourth century BCE—all combined to produce an astounding surge in national prosperity.

However, within a century of the Northern Song founding, official complacency and corruption began to set in. Also, newer generations of men, particularly from the south, beneficiaries of the educational opportunities that prosperity and government policy had created, began passing the civil service examinations in large numbers and also began challenging the honesty and competence of top officialdom. The first wave of these men was born around the year 1000. The means through which they sought to exert themselves was not management expertise, but rather classical learning, moral refinement, and critical judgment. They were the champions of a Confucian revival, commonly called Neo-Confucianism, that originated in the late Tang (as noted earlier) and was now resumed, to deepen and spread through the whole remainder of the Song period and beyond.

The new men, many of them southern Confucian revivalists, demanded reforms, and their reform demands escalated over the years as a sense of unresolved crisis in national security mounted with the Song's chronic inability to overpower the Liao and Xi Xia. This led to the astounding remaking of Song government conducted by the southern degree-holder and chief minister Wang Anshi during the years from 1067 to 1085. "Enrich the state, strengthen the army" was the slogan. With the warm support of Emperor Shenzong, Wang justified on Confucian grounds a holistic vision of an all-powerful state by developing through commentary an update of the classic *Rites of Zhou*, a text last seen put to use for reform purposes by Su Chuo in the sixth century. Wang's idea was that government should have a direct hand in fostering economic growth nationwide, and that the revenues derived from enhanced growth should then sustain a greatly improved military capability. Much of this "New Policies" program was accomplished using special task forces and new revenue sources that bypassed a largely hostile regular bureaucracy. By 1082, Wang's Council of State had charge of finance, personnel, military planning and operations; mining and metallurgy; salt and tea production; rural credit; and wholesale interregional and international sea trade. A land resurvey was ordered for north China. A national militia was developed to replace eventually the huge, expensive, and ineffective professional army inherited from the Five Dynasties. The examination system was completely retooled to include a national school system whose curriculum was based in Wang's "New Studies." This curriculum heavily discouraged the study of history, and criticism and debate were not welcome. Wang's critics grounded their dislike of the New Policies in their comprehensive and detailed study of China's history. Many conservative opponents of Wang were dismissed, or resigned, or retired in exile to Luoyang.

Uppermost in Shenzong's mind was the purpose of all this reform: enhanced Song military leverage over the Liao and Xi Xia—and indeed everywhere else along the Song land frontier, including Sichuan, the Dali kingdom in Yunnan, and a now independent

Annam (Vietnam). Fights with the Liao and Xi Xia in the 1040s had gone badly and had ended in the payment of increased Song subsidies to both. Only occasionally allied, the Liao and Xi Xia more often fought each other, which helped to create opportunities for Song aggression against the weaker party, the Xi Xia. Song-Liao hostility over border demarcation flared up from 1074 to 1076 but was settled by negotiation. The Song and Xi Xia had never agreed on a common border, and Song annexationist wars over border territory, which broke out three times in the 1080s and 1090s, escalated into disastrous attempts to destroy the Xi Xia state altogether. Wang was in favor of deferring war until his reforms were further advanced. It was Shenzong, in combination with palace eunuchs, hereditary military generals, and hawkish civilian officials all looking for career advancement, who agitated for war.

Shenzong died in 1085. A regency, headed by the dowager empress from 1085 until her death in 1093, sponsored the removal of the partisans of the New Policies and their replacement by a loose grouping of conservative opponents, among them such famous names as Su Shi, Sima Guang, and Cheng Yi. Many of the New Policies were rescinded. Aggression against the Liao and Xi Xia was toned down.

Then, during the reigns of Zhezong (to 1100) and Huizong (1100–1125), yet a final partisan turnover brought on the restoration of the New Policies faction, the blacklisting of some three hundred officials of the conservative opposition, and the suppression of all internal protest and policy debate. Chief minister Cai Jing ran the government for many years. When old age diminished the chief minister's vigor, Huizong relied more and more on palace eunuch Tong Guan. The reformists not only revived much of Wang's centrally directed program, but went even further. They expanded a costly nationwide system of schools that came to enroll some two hundred thousand students, all following a New Policies curriculum that dropped poetry and history to focus on Wang's Confucian commentaries, Huizong's commentaries on the Daoist classics, and the Song legal code. The reformists also put into effect programs that made the central state something of a national welfare agency: poorhouses, clinics, and free cemeteries absorbed unknown but possibly large outlays of revenue. The late Northern Song was thus a kind of brief golden age, and the emperor who presided over it was a cultural impresario, with deep personal interests in architecture, garden\ building, painting, calligraphy, music, medicine, and Daoism.

But there was another side to the Northern Song. From 1116, when the eunuch Tong was appointed to the Council of State, the dynasty resumed the aggressive military stance it had assumed earlier under Shenzong. The Liao confederation in the north began unraveling in the early 1100s, wracked both by tribal rebellions and by murderous intrigues at court. From 1112, and over the next decade, the Jurchen tribes of northern Manchuria, led by Aguda, conducted a series of fierce wars against the Liao, conquered more and more Liao territory, and declared itself the Jin ("Gold") dynasty in 1115. The Song court, thanks to its many envoys to the Liao and Jin, was well aware of these developments, and, prodded by Tong, unwisely decided to turn the Liao distress to its own advantage and negotiate an agreement with Aguda, so that the Song might then recapture the sixteen prefectures lost to the Liao in 937. However, the Song army, partly because it was distracted at this time by war with the Xi Xia and by the dangerous Fang La rebellion in Zhejiang, performed wretchedly in its attack on the Liao. Aguda destroyed the Liao on his own and captured the sixteen prefectures, a fait accompli the Song had to accede to in 1123. That such a blunder could happen has been attributed to the silencing of all internal debate that the Northern Song reform faction had long imposed.

What came next was fatal for the Northern Song. In the autumn of 1125, for reasons that are not clear, the Jin invaded north China in force and besieged Kaifeng. The siege was lifted diplomatically, but only after the Song court agreed to ruinous terms. There followed a complete turnabout in central government. Under the leadership of chief minister Li Gang (1083–1140), the officials persuaded Huizong to abdicate in favor of his son, known posthumously as Qinzong. A dramatic demonstration by patriotic students of the national university helped bring about the execution of Tong Guan and the removal of other influential eunuchs as well. The reform faction, discredited by its yielding to Jin demands, was turned out of office. The Song, hoping to rely on newly recruited militias, rejected the agreement with the Jin and vowed to stand and fight. They had no time to prepare, however, and the Jin invaded again. Kaifeng fell in January 1127. The Jin army thoroughly plundered it. Huizong, Qinzong, and nearly the entire imperial household, numbering in the thousands, were marched off in captivity to Manchuria. A Song imperial prince, Gaozong, managed to head a new government that eventually decided, for safety reasons, to relocate south, not to Nanjing, but to Hangzhou, as a "temporary capital." Thus was founded the Southern Song dynasty (1127–1279). Inconclusive wars with the Jin over control of north and central China continued until 1142. Tripartite East Asia consisted now of the Jin (with a much larger presence in north China than the Liao had had), Southern Song, and Xi Xia.

The Jin (1115–1234), Xi Xia (982–1227), and Southern Song (1127–1279)

The Song dynasty lost a third of its territory with its relocation to south China. The central government had to be built again from the beginning. The military likewise had to be completely reconstituted, mainly by recruiting former bandit armies. Fundamental national security policy—whether to try to retake north China or remain quietly in the south as a Jin vassal state—was never conclusively determined but shifted this way and that until the very end, the Mongol conquest of the 1270s.

The Jurchen Jin, too, were divided over fundamental policy. Divisive issues of cultural identity also troubled the regime. The Jin was heavily committed to north China, and partly for that reason it was less able than the Liao to control Inner Asia. The Tangut Xi Xia state found itself cut off from the Southern Song, owing to the Jin conquest of north China. In this circumstance, the Xi Xia became less warlike and focused its efforts on internal development. Like the Jin, it was a multiethnic state, but with a more effective policy of managing interethnic relations. With a nod to the Tibetans, the Xi Xia became a Tantric Buddhist theocracy; with a nod to the Chinese, it simultaneously developed Confucian institutions and civil service examinations. Great efforts were made to translate Buddhist scripture and classic Chinese texts into Tangut. A massive

Tangut-language law code combined Tang law with Tangut tribal tradition. But despite this cultural efflorescence, Xi Xia isolation and withdrawal more and more left the Jin and Southern Song in a two-way power standoff in East Asia.

The Jin made deep but unsuccessful probes south across the Yangzi in pursuit of Gaozong and other key surviving members of the Song imperial family, but the conquest of the south, and the unification of China under Jin rule, was never the Jin's driving ambition. It was difficult enough for the Jin to consolidate its hold on the forty million Chinese in the north. Eventually, Jurchen and other fighters and their families, perhaps some six million people, were moved from Manchuria and resettled in special military colonies in north China.

In 1142 the fighting ended, and a peace agreement between the Jin and Song was reached. This came about after the Jin had seriously mishandled the many defections of Song generals, armies, and civil officials, and after Gaozong had disposed of the irredentists on his side, especially the loyalist general Yue Fei and the leading councilor, Zhao Ding. The agreement heavily favored the Jin. The two sides recognized the Huai River as their common border. The Song agreed to send annual subventions in silk and silver. It also agreed to accept an inferior posture of vassalage to the Jin, a concession it did not advertise at home. This was a shaky peace. The resumption of war always remained open as an option for political factions in both empires.

In the Jin case, the war issue was connected in a complex way with a problem that had earlier vexed the Liao: how far to preserve tribal ways, and how far to change or end them in the interest of Chinese-style autocratic and bureaucratic state building? The tensions here led to appallingly bloody acts. In 1147, Emperor Xizong (not to be confused with the Tang emperor also called Xizong) murdered 48 former Liao Chinese officials; in 1150, Xizong's cousin, usurper Wanyan Liang (Prince Hailing), killed Xizong, 72 male members of the imperial family, and large numbers of the Jurchen elite. Wanyan Liang stood on the Chinese side of the issue. From 1150 to 1161, the new ruler moved most of the Jin ruling apparatus out of Manchuria into north China and built a new capital on the site of present-day Beijing as well as a southern capital at Kaifeng. Then, he amassed a huge army and navy, and in 1161 he took personal command of an all-out invasion of the Southern Song. This was an act not of considered policy, but of megalomania. The Khitans and others refused to join in. In December 1161, just after his forces reached but failed to cross the Yangzi, officers acting on behalf of imperial clan moderates murdered Wanyan Liang. That ended the attempted conquest and annexation.

Jin China reached its apogee during the long and generally peaceful reign of Shizong (Wanyan Wulu, r. 1161–1189), who cancelled the attack on the Southern Song and in 1165 agreed to a new treaty, this one less favorable to the Jin than the treaty of 1142 had been. By 1207, a very large, perhaps bloated government of some forty-seven thousand officials ruled north China (under Wang Anshi, Northern Song bureaucracy had expanded to thirty-four thousand officials in 1086). Jurchen tribal aristocrats dominated the top positions, while Chinese, recruited through a much-expanded national Confucian school system and civil service examinations, filled most of the rest of the positions. Former Liao Chinese were given advantages over former Song Chinese. Jurchen customs, language, and script were heavily promoted. Tribal consultative procedures, featuring votes and formal head counts, were reintroduced at court. During the reigns of Zhangzong (1190–1208) and Xuanzong (1213–1224) there was extended debate and votes taken on the troublesome question of Jin dynastic identity. Just where did the Jin fit in China's historical sequence? Did the sequence go from Tang to Liao to Jin, or Tang via a gap to Jin? What about the Northern Song? Was it the Jin mission, then, to carry on Tang traditions and to deny cultural legitimacy either to the Liao or the Song? The debates took place off and on from 1194 to 1214. No definitive conclusion was ever reached. The Jin never gained a sure corporate sense of itself.

New Developments in the Southern Song

Like the An Lushan rebellion of 755–763, the Jurchen invasion of 1126 and the Song evacuation of north China was a watershed event, a great breaking point in history. The traumatic reduction of

Song China to a southern rump changed many things, some concretely, some symbolically. Politically, it discredited the centrally directed New Policies reform programs of Wang Anshi and Cai Jing. While in the north under Jin rule, the Chinese literati were on the whole content to follow the traditional literary standards of the Tang, in south China under the Southern Song there developed an intense and many-sided debate about the whole future direction of China's civilization. The examination system in both north and south turned out many more graduates than the bureaucracy needed. The Jin responded by creating more bureaucratic positions. The Southern Song did not, and so there emerged in south China an elite society that was strongly localist and unconnected to Hangzhou, as well as a sizable Confucian intelligentsia that was deeply concerned for the future of China but only loosely involved with the central state. One of the leading figures was Zhu Xi (1130–1200). Zhu won his *jinshi* degree (the highest degree) in 1148 at the very young age of eighteen, although he spent most of his life not in office, but pursuing his own agenda of reforming China. This was an ambition as all-encompassing as Wang Anshi's, but now no longer involving the central state but rather the Confucian intelligentsia, in office or out, as the leading engine of change. In the field of philosophy, Zhu singled out and annotated the so-called Four Books (in preference to the Five Classics) as the core curriculum for education; identified an orthodox line of correct transmitters of the Confucian doctrines down through time; and elaborated a metaphysics that at last displaced Buddhism as the ultimate explainer of all cosmic and human existence. In the area of institutions, he helped shape the intelligentsia into a national Confucian fellowship focused upon ethical self-cultivation and leadership over local institutions: the privately funded academy, the community compact, the community granary, and the local militia. The functions of these institutions had earlier been included in the central agenda of the Song state. As for the central state, Zhu would make it the creature of the Confucian fellowship—the overall guardian of the new Confucian order and a passive recipient of moral and political advice, rather than a free agent. This complex of ideas was commonly referred to as *daoxue*—"the learning of the way." Its opponents called it "specialized learning," "private theories," and even "false learning."

The Southern Song state, meanwhile, wavered, as did the Jin, between war policies and peace policies. In the summer of 1206 it formally declared war and launched a northern invasion that soon bogged down in wet weather, logistical mishaps, and incompetent command. A hoped-for revolt of Jurchen-ruled Chinese never materialized. Peace negotiations in 1208 forced the Song to raise its annual payments. The war faction, thoroughly discredited, was thrown out of office. The severed head of its leader was sent in a lacquer box to the Jin. Neither contestant could foresee in the Mongol confederation of Chinggis Khan, just then emerging, its own imminent demise and the rise of a wholly new East Asian system of power.

The End of Tripartition

Battered by unremitting natural disasters (including the catastrophic 1194 flood of the Yellow River), and beset by lethal power struggles at court, the Jin dynasty began slowly to fall apart. From 1206, Chinese warlords created separatist regimes in Shandong. Around the same time, a revived Khitan Liao state came to power in central Manchuria. A separate Jurchen state, its founder committed to the Daoist religion, formed in northern and eastern Manchuria in 1215. In addition to all this, annual Mongol raids into north China began in 1211. In 1215, the Jin court felt compelled for safety reasons to move its capital south to Kaifeng. The Mongols then captured the Jin central capital (Zhongdu, present-day Beijing).

Until almost the very end, the three powers sharing the Chinese cultural landscape were more preoccupied with one another than with the Mongols. There was a Xi Xia attack on a weakened Jin in 1217, along with a series of Jin attacks on the Southern Song. Finally, the last Jin ruler, Aizong (r. 1223–1234), his territory having shrunk to Henan, Shaanxi, and parts of Shandong and Shanxi, concluded peace on equal terms with both the Song in 1224 and the Xi Xia in 1225. But in 1227 the Mongols destroyed and annexed the Xi Xia. A yearlong Mongol siege of Kaifeng (1232–1233) ended in Aizong's flight south and suicide. Early in 1234, the Jin dynasty was no more, and the Mongols controlled all of north China.

The Southern Song court for a long time saw the Mongol attacks less as a threat than as an opportunity to defeat the Jin and recover north China for themselves. The court made alliances with the separatist warlords in Shandong. In 1233, Song emperor Lizong agreed to contribute twenty thousand troops and a large quantity of provisions to the final Mongol assault on the Jin. Then, unpersuaded by arguments that Henan was too depopulated and economically ruined by years of war to sustain a Song annexation, Lizong sent his armies north. After eight weeks, the Mongols routed them at Luoyang. So ended the long, sad story of Southern Song irredentism.

Still, for over forty years, the Southern Song maintained a defense against Mongol-ruled north China. During that time, the court took a series of steps, ending in 1241, to make the Zhu Xi school of *daoxue* official state orthodoxy. This was an effort at moral rearmament, a Song attempt to universalize on spiritual grounds what could no longer be unified militarily. The decision was also prompted by the Mongols' official sponsorship of Confucian study and by their one-off revival of the civil service examinations.

The standoff with the Mongols began to go badly for the Song in the 1250s and 1260s, as the Mongols came to understand that siege machinery and naval forces were going to be the keys to military success on the battlefronts of China. The Mongols' six-year siege of Xiangyang on the Han River ended in 1273 with the defection of the defending Song generals and their armies. In the Southern Song capital at Hangzhou, a controversial finance expert of military origins, Jia Sidao, was appointed chief minister of state in 1259, a position he held until dismissed in March 1275. His policy of paying for defense by ruthlessly confiscating large landholdings in the Yangzi delta area kindled such anger among high officials and many Confucian literati that they blamed him, rather unfairly, for the Song collapse.

Unlike the Mongols' conquest of north China, the advance of Mongol-led armies into south China involved minimal bloodshed and destruction. Hangzhou was entered peacefully. The Song court rejected the urgings of some to mount an all-out defense. The empress dowager and the child emperor surrendered early in 1276. They were transported to the Mongol capital, Dadu (now Beijing), and were treated well there. That was not quite the end, however.

Two infant princes and their supporters fled south by sea while the greatest celebrity of the day, the number-one *jinshi* degree-holder Wen Tianxiang, mounted a hopeless but symbolically important loyalist act of resistance against the Mongols in Jiangxi. Wen was defeated and captured in 1278; and because he refused to capitulate, he was executed in Dadu in 1283. Meanwhile, a Mongol-commandeered fleet destroyed the last of the fleeing Song court off Canton in 1279. The Song mandate was thus extinguished. The Song legacy, not of institutionalized power, but of Neo-Confucianism and loyalism, lived on.

PART 4

Permanent Unity Largely Achieved: Yuan, Ming, and Qing

The last span of history to be covered in this book consists of the Yuan, Ming, and Qing to 1850, a period of nearly six hundred years during which only three dynasties, ruling one after the other, and despite their great differences, built a durable institutional framework for the governance of China sufficient to hold the country together under central control most of the time, and, in the Yuan and Qing, added considerable extra-Chinese territory to it. The question is, how did these regimes, which were by no means carbon copies, manage to achieve such an impressive record of stability?

One symptom of the new stability was the choice of a permanent site for the capital city, built (and rebuilt) at an eccentric spot in the northeast, where it has remained to the present day under the name Beijing. Chang'an, Luoyang, Kaifeng, Hangzhou, and Nanjing, capitals of past regimes, including long-lived dynasties such as the Han and Tang, yielded to Beijing, a place without deep historical resonances, located on the fringe of Inner Asia, and first built up by non-Chinese regimes, the Liao and Jin. The Ming founder chose Nanjing, but his son, the Yongle emperor, rebuilt Beijing and moved the capital back there in 1421.

The ruling houses—Mongol, Chinese, and Manchu—all came to power after first waging all-out war to win the mandate of Heaven, sweeping every competitor from the field. Many of the preceding dynasties had been founded by coups d'état: the Song by a military mutiny; the Tang similarly. A tradition of dynastic abdication (*shanrang*) made possible in some cases a bloodless turnover of ruling houses. Founding a dynasty on the back of victory in all-out war seems to have lent a formidable aura of legitimacy to the Yuan, Ming, and Qing. (That the Yuan collapsed as soon as it did came as a bit of a surprise, but dynasties such as the Qin and Sui that reunified China after long periods of division seem for various reasons to have experienced short life spans. Still, the Qin lasted fifteen years, the Sui twenty-nine, and the Yuan eighty-eight.)

The Mongols and their Chinese advisers at the outset ignored Song institutions and drew heavily upon Liao, Jin, and ultimately Tang precedents to construct a governing system for a reunited China. The main Yuan effect upon the complexion of Ming and Qing institutions appears to have been the idea, not originated but certainly emphasized by the Mongols, that control of such a huge empire required that distinct lines of separation needed to be drawn between palace and bureaucracy, between civil society and a hereditary military, and between and among ethnic, occupational, and regional groups in bureaucracy and society at large. The Yuan also carved China up into large provinces, much of whose geographical shape survives to the present day. In the Yuan, the Censorate became a distinct and occasionally powerful organ of political protest as well as of surveillance over the rest of the bureaucracy. A few Southern Song arrangements were added later, at the expense of northern tradition; most important, Zhu Xi's Neo-Confucianism was singled out as China's premier unifying ideology and as the basis for a revived national system of competitive written examinations qualifying candidates for office holding. Restricted quotas ensured that the potentially powerful influence of degree-winners was counterbalanced by officials with other kinds of qualifications; tight quotas were also responsible for extending from Song times the continued fostering of a very large community of students and educated men, literati who had little hope of entering government and were therefore normally engaged in family, teaching, and other local matters, but who in times of crisis served as an articulate national intelligentsia. The Ming founders, despite their anti-Mongol ethnic posturing, clearly built their dynasty on these Yuan foundations.

The most pressing problem the Yuan bequeathed to its Ming successor was the evident shakiness of its central structure of control.

Was the problem the structure, or the officials who staffed it, or both? The founding emperor of the Ming and the literati who advised him constantly talked about why the Yuan had collapsed and caused seventeen years of anarchy and horror for all the people of China. For them, understanding the Yuan collapse was a prerequisite to building safeguards sufficient to prevent a similar collapse of the new Ming order. It is this intellectual edge to the Ming founding that differentiates it from its predecessors in the Chinese past that have been discussed thus far. Major dynastic founders, men such as those who founded the Tang and Northern Song, were by and large pragmatic actors who had their advisers, to be sure, but certainly were not surrounded, as the Ming founder was, by a militant and mobilized community of scholarly ideologues from south China's Zhejiang province, men who were versed in Neo-Confucianism, history, and current events and who were able and eager to lay out a comprehensive agenda for the new Ming state.

The Ming founders' analysis of the Yuan collapse was subtle and complex, but also impassioned and driven by their own political needs. At the outset, they found no single issue adequate to explain it, but rather a tissue of causes having something to do with Yuan institutions, more to do with the dominant positions of non-Chinese elites, but most of all to do with ethical anomie, administrative laxity, and corruption on the part of nearly everyone holding official positions high and low. Further, it was especially Chinese officials in Yuan government whom they found guilty of corruption and malfeasance on such a scale as to give the masses of the people of China little choice but to rise up in nationwide rebellion. All of the Ming builders had witnessed one or more aspects of this corruption. Zhu Yuanzhang, the ex-peasant and founding emperor (known posthumously as Ming Taizu), made some vivid statements of his own about what he as a youth had seen of corruption and incompetence in Yuan local government. Things had gotten to such a sorry state not because the Mongols were cruel, but because, in Taizu's view, they were negligent. At court, the emperors had allowed power to drift downward into the hands of prime ministers who then denied the emperor any real role in governance and on their own ran the great Yuan empire by means of favoritism and bribery.

The Zhejiang Confucian intelligentsia, welcomed by the Ming founder into his developing regime as early as 1360, also had direct personal experiences of the evils of Yuan local government, and they drew from these experiences conclusions that were quite compatible with Taizu's. They were older than the unschooled Taizu, and, as educated men, they had earlier tried to reform from below the whole Yuan system. They had enlisted the support of sympathetic Yuan officials (some of them non-Chinese) who were serving in Zhejiang, in the cause of achieving distributive fairness in the imposition of service obligations on large and small households, a difficult task that required breaking the corrupt linkages between large and rich households and greedy officials and clerks in local government. Such reforms were indeed launched, with great intensity, in a cloud of Confucian moral propaganda, but in the end they failed because the regional censors could not be persuaded to endorse them. And so, things drifted. Instead of mobilizing forces to suppress great outlaws such as the pirate Fang Guozhen, Yuan central government offered them titles and rewards to buy their loyalty. The Ming founders were determined to put a permanent end to this pattern and, generally speaking, they did just that.

No earlier dynasty was ever founded quite as the Ming was, and there is no doubt but that Taizu and his advisers seized upon the eradication of local corruption and replaced it with honest government for the sake of all the people as the energizing and legitimizing aim of their many efforts. As for overthrowing the Yuan, the Ming founders considered it a legitimate dynasty, and they never claimed responsibility for its destruction. No, they argued; the Yuan forfeited the empire on its own initiative. What the Ming conquered and destroyed was not the Yuan, but the various Chinese and other warlords who had come to power in the wake of the Yuan downfall. But establishing clean and honest government in early Ming China proved to be a most frustrating task. It required nothing less than huge and bloody purges of everyone suspected of corruption or treason in officialdom, and the reeducation of all the people of China in basic Confucian morality. It also required some institutional reconfiguring of the inherited Yuan machinery of government, extinguishing all prime ministerial functions at the provincial and central levels, with a view to giving the emperor unrestricted personal access to every available lever of power—and all this because the moral rot prevalent in Yuan times had eaten so deeply into the minds of even China's educated elites and highest officials that they could not be trusted with unchecked and unsupervised responsibilities of any kind.

There exists much debate in China and abroad over whether Taizu was a good and effective ruler—a protonationalist who expelled the Mongols, unified China, and ruled it well—or an evil influence whose chief legacy was a machinery of centralized despotism that placed such a straitjacket on China that centuries later it could barely respond to the challenges of the modern world, and who reinforced an authoritarianism whose effects linger to the present day. The answer appears to be that he was both, or neither. The power of his legacy is hard to gauge, for two reasons. One, every new emperor in the Ming, beginning with Taizu's own grandson and immediate successor, the Jianwen emperor, felt free to shake off the supposed straitjacket and make changes in the inherited institutions and lines of policy. And two, Taizu ruled so long (thirty years), issued so many edicts and directives, and penned so much himself that his written legacy was so riddled with contradictions that much of it was simply ignored, or it was selectively invoked by political actors in later times to support almost any position they might choose. At the same time, it is also the case that the gross institutional features of Ming government were adopted by its successor, the Qing, and the Qing rulers were always respectful of the Ming founder and protective of his reputation. But it might be better said that the Qing institutions for the governing of China were based upon a much deeper inheritance reaching back to Yuan, Tang, and Han times and earlier. Perhaps Taizu's principal contribution was his removal of permanent, regularly appointed prime ministerial positions at the central and provincial levels.

A leading example of the ambiguities in Taizu's legacy is his position on the role of eunuchs. He is on record as having sternly advised that palace eunuchs be kept few in number, that they be forbidden to learn to read and write, and that their duties be restricted to the menial. But in fact, he ignored his own advice and found eunuchs useful in military supervision and in the conduct of border trade and foreign relations. From the time of the Yongle emperor's usurpation in 1402, palace eunuchs began to proliferate and to develop their own recruitment modes, schools, and system of internal ranking and controls. By the late Ming, the eunuch corps had become much larger than the civil bureaucracy, numbering a hundred thousand or more in Beijing, Nanjing, and many other parts of China, where eunuchs handled military and police functions, managed imperial farms, collected special taxes, and managed salt production, mining, and silk manufacture in addition to their earlier roles in foreign trade and diplomacy. In Beijing, they acted as the emperors' personal office staff (in addition to performing their culinary and many other services); they also substituted for the emperor in the highest-level review of legal appeals and court cases. In some cases eunuchs became very rich, patronized other eunuchs, formed links with the north China criminal underworld, and headed families of their own by adoption. It is noteworthy that they never managed to seize control of the throne in the Ming as they did in the late Tang. To the end, Ming eunuch power remained fragile, and emperors could and did punish and kill them almost at will. Just as there was no executive prime minister in charge of the regular bureaucracy, there was no regular chief eunuch's office either. Unless found in the general principle of the primacy of imperial authority in any conceivable context, Taizu's supposed legacy regarding restrictions on eunuchs was nowhere to be found in this situation.

In this connection, it is sometimes overlooked that both the Ming and Qing had what amounts to a third branch of government that was associated personally with the emperor and functioned separately from the civil and military hierarchies. The Ming-style palace eunuch corps was continued in the very early Qing, but it came to be argued that eunuchs had had a major role in causing the deterioration and collapse of the Ming. Eunuch factions and factions in the regular bureaucracy had repeatedly made cooperative arrangements with a view to destroying their respective rivals. So, in 1661 the decision was taken to drastically reduce the size and curtail the functions of the eunuchs, and to supplant them with the many imperial bondservants (*booi*) that had accompanied the Manchu conquest machine into China. Thus the Imperial Household Department (Neiwufu) came into being, with the remaining small corps of eunuchs placed under its supervision. From an original staff of 402, by 1796 the department numbered 1,623. It was a self-contained bureaucracy, with its own schools and testing procedures, with censors and bureaus that resembled those of the Six Ministries of the civil bureaucracy. Revenue was the most important bureau; it controlled a kind of conglomerate imperial enterprise encompassing commerce and industry, especially involving ginseng, copper, salt, silk, textiles, and foreign trade, much like its Ming eunuch predecessor. By the eighteenth century, the Imperial Household Department had grown extremely corrupt. However, it never controlled the flow of documents between emperor and bureaucracy, nor did it have the military and police capabilities of the Ming eunuchs.

The Yuan situation appears to have been different. There were many revenue-producing agencies based in the Yuan capital that were under nominal imperial control, but the later Yuan emperors were mainly creatures of high-level Mongol or Turkish grandee factions. The leaders of these factions controlled military-guard units, and they routinely seized the revenue-producing agencies for personal or factional use whenever they came to power. In this respect, the Ming and Qing represent a distinct upward leap in imperial command.

The early Ming profile, at court and in the country at large, was very different from the situation in the early Qing. A list of comparisons can show this: Manchus from the northeast, outside China proper, founded the Qing; Chinese from the center and south created the Ming. Ming military unification was accomplished relatively swiftly—over about eight years, from 1360, when Taizu established his capital in Nanjing, to 1368, when Ming forces entered the Yuan capital, Dadu , and forced the Yuan imperial court to retreat to Mongolia; the Qing required some forty years, from 1644 to 1683, to defeat all its former military allies and unify China proper. But the Ming's Taizu had an easier time of it—the Yuan loyalism he faced was weak, and his warlord opponents put up little in the way of fierce, diehard resistance to him. It was much harder going for the Manchus. While defections and capitulations to the Manchus were commonplace, there were also major urban pockets of suicidal Ming loyalism and local pride, led by Chinese literati, especially in the south, the like of which was last seen in Wen Tianxiang's late thirteenth-century resistance to the Mongol conquest. Ming Taizu never had to face such obstacles; the

Qing takeover was, for that and other reasons, much more violent. Ming Taizu was alert to the need to discipline and punish unruly troops, and the wars of Ming unification evidenced fairly little in the way of massacres, plunder, and wanton wreckage; there were no early Ming counterparts to the Manchu massacres of whole populations in a half-dozen big south China cities, including the infamous slaughter and destruction at Yangzhou in May 1645 (where much of the actual killing was done not by Manchu, but by Chinese troops), and even the Mongol conquest of south China was peaceful by contrast. Nor did the Yuan or Ming founders, Khubilai or Taizu, find it necessary to conduct a national headcount of all supporters and resisters, as the Manchus did, when in June 1645 they imposed the requirement that all Chinese males show their new loyalty by adopting the Manchu coiffure of a shaved forehead and rear-hanging pigtail. Taizu's violent streak manifested itself after he unified China; the Manchus, by contrast, eased up after the unification was complete.

It is interesting, too, to note the very different things leading intellectuals were saying about the condition and the future of China in the seventeenth century as compared to the fourteenth. In the fourteenth century, the Zhejiang intellectuals who gathered around Taizu and advised him had already thought hard about the future of China and, generally speaking, found solutions to the Yuan breakdown and subsequent disorders in the building up of emperor-centered power, institutionally untrammeled and guided only by ethical constraints, strong enough to impose by diktat whatever remedies—penal, educational, bureaucratic—were required to cleanse and reorient the minds of all the people of China and return the civilization to something approaching its Golden Age state of grace. The leading seventeenth-century intellectuals were quite different. Gu Yanwu (1613–1682), Huang Zongxi (1610–1695), and others were personally involved not in the Qing conquest, but in the failed southern Ming resistance. The fourteenth-century intellectuals located the source of the trouble in a nationwide epidemic of self-centered greed and corruption; and indeed, this approach was endorsed in the seventeenth-century courts of the Shunzhi and Kangxi emperors, with the first focused on suppressing corruption of all sorts, and the second on educating all the people of China in fundamental Confucian values. But the seventeenth-century intellectuals, who thought long and hard, as their fourteenth-century colleagues had, about what had gone wrong with China, did not trace the troubles to corruption, and corruption to mental or spiritual failures. Both Huang and Gu were chary of Song Neo-Confucian orthodoxy, but Gu went further to emphasize the value of evidentiary research and resurrect Han dynasty thinkers as sources closer to the original Confucianism. Neither Huang nor Gu liked centering the discussion of China's troubles on minds and mentalities, and they looked instead to the desirability of reworking institutions. (Huang and Gu knew each other, read each other's work, and were agreed upon many issues.) Huang thought the Ming emperors had had too much authority and had abused it, and so he proposed that imperial authority be shared with a restored prime minister; and since the Ming system of creating intrabureaucratic jurisdictional conflict as a means of sustaining central control appeared counterproductive, Huang would further apportion discretionary authority all down the line to include the county magistrates. Both Huang and Gu wanted to abolish the apparatus of provincial and circuit supervision that every post–An Lushan dynasty, including the Ming, had placed between the center and the localities. Still, the case remains that however much admired their reform ideas were in literati circles, they had virtually no impact on the Qing rulers, who were on the whole content to rule China by working within the inherited and familiar Ming institutional format.

The Ming was, then, exceptional in making common cause with a militant and visionary wing of the Confucian intelligentsia during its founding phase. And what of the Mongols? The Mongols had important commitments in other parts of the world, and it was not until the 1250s and 1260s that Khubilai, while still a young regional prince, called in northern Chinese Confucians to assist him in creating appropriate machinery for ruling China and to cultivate support in educated circles throughout China for his drive toward supreme power. Northern Confucians such as Xu Heng (1209–1281) also played an important part in familiarizing young Mongols and Central Asians at court in the psychological ("mind-and-heart") basics of Confucian doctrine. The Manchus had less need of all that, being all along more familiar with Ming civilization than the Mongols were with the Jin or Southern Song, and having consistently had their attention much more heavily focused on China. Indeed, Ming defectors and educated Chinese natives of Manchuria were from the beginning prominent participants in the rise of the Qing, whereas ethnic Chinese had scarcely any role at all in the critical early phases of the creation of the Mongol empire. Although none of the early Qing rulers bothered to search out a Confucian ideological vanguard and make common cause with it in the style of Ming Taizu, they certainly made practical use of advisers such as the Manchurian Chinese Fan Wencheng (1597–1666) in reconstituting Ming-style institutions for the ruling of China.

It is time now to take a closer look at the Yuan, Ming, and Qing, providers of nearly seven centuries of unity and relatively stable rule, the longest such span China ever experienced.

Yuan China
1271–1368

The Mongol empire was unprecedented in its geographical scale. China had never seen anything quite like it. Earlier "barbarian" regimes, such as those founded by the Khitans, the Jurchens, or, earlier, the Tuobas, had all been heavily involved with north China and its cultural and administrative heritage. This was much less the case with the Mongols. From Chinggis Khan's time down to the rise of his grandson Khubilai in the 1260s, the Mongols, their power center still located in the steppes, were also attracted to Transoxania, Iran, the Middle East, and the Volga and Caucasus regions. For fifty years, the Mongols did not even bother to declare a Chinese-style dynasty in north China—until, in 1271, Khubilai's Chinese advisers persuaded him to declare one, the Yuan.

The effect of Mongol raiding and warfare in north China appears to have been catastrophic. In 1207, the Jin could count some 50 million people; from 1234 to 1236, the Mongol authorities found but 8.5 million. Early Mongol rule in heavily battered north China featured at the local level a complicated mix of Chinese warlords, former Jin officials, and Buddhist and Daoist priests serving as community leaders. At higher levels, governance reflected the Mongols' stunning ability to commandeer administrative and technical expertise from all parts of their Eurasian empire. Thus, Muslim finance and tax experts were fetched from Transoxania and put to work in north China, where they imposed their own techniques and often ignored China's administrative traditions (*Hanfa*). Similarly, administrators from China were put to work in Transoxania. North China was squeezed as a resource base for Mongol operations worldwide. Other than that, it held no special importance for the Mongols.

It was Khubilai who changed things. A different approach was shown in the north China appanage of young prince Khubilai (1215–1294), where his mother, a Nestorian Christian, proved to be a good manager. Her and Khubilai's princely court became a magnet for Confucian intellectuals and others in north China who were desperately seeking someone among the Mongol elite whom they could support and, as advisers and operatives, influence in such a way as to restore some semblance of traditional normality to the dreadful state of affairs in their once-flourishing homeland. As it turned out, Khubilai was ambitious to succeed his elder brother Möngke as "great khan" of the Mongol empire; if Chinese Confucians could help him in his drive for power, well and good. Khubilai flattered them, and his Chinese adherents did everything they could to rally support behind Khubilai's seizure of power from 1260 to 1264. In the 1270s, they worked hard to convince the southern Chinese of the legitimacy of the khan-emperor's attempt at the conquest and annexation of the Southern Song.

The tripartite power competition that for three centuries had commanded the scene in East Asia was at last over, thanks to Khubilai's successful plan to secede from the overstretched Mongol world empire and build a China-centered Mongol empire of his own. The destruction of the Xi Xia and Dali states and the various Manchurian entities, and the incorporation of their territories into the Yuan realm, created an enlarged lebensraum for China proper, as the Yuan government opened the annexed territories to Chinese immigration.

But after the 1279 conquest of the Southern Song, Khubilai ceased his close cooperation with his Confucian officials and advisers, leaned instead upon his mainly Muslim fiscal experts, and made of Yuan China a gigantic resource base for further expansion in Asia: Burma (1277, 1287), Vietnam (1281, 1285, 1287), Japan (1274, 1281), and Java (1292). There were also long and expensive wars against other Mongol khanates to the west over control of Xinjiang and Mongolia (in the end, the Yuan kept Mongolia and ceded Xinjiang). All these thrusts were costly and unproductive, and Khubilai's grandson and successor, Temür, after about 1300, put an end to all further expansion.

Given that there were not many Mongols (perhaps seven hundred thousand warriors), and given that most of China is not good territory for mounted warfare in the nomad style, there is no accounting for the astounding Yuan success in unifying China unless one recognizes the Mongols' aptitude, perhaps derived from animal herding, for commandeering the efforts and skills of others. In addition, the Mongols had a willingness to tolerate, and indeed patronize, the philosophies and religions of the people they conquered. The conquest of south China called not for cavalry maneuvers, but for naval forces and sieges; and as for sieges, the Mongols brought into China from the Muslim world experts in the new ballistic machines, counterweighted trebuchets, and put them to use in the siege of Xiangyang. For navies, the Mongols commandeered Korean and Song fleets for maritime operations, among other measures. The military manpower used in the conquest of south China consisted mainly of Chinese armies under Mongol command. Defectors were, on the whole, welcomed and well treated. Although wary of Chinese cultural power, the early Mongols were not afraid of it and used imported Turks, Muslims, and Tibetan Buddhists as alternative sources of administrative talent.

Yuan rule over China became exceedingly complex, a confusing amalgam of religious, occupational, and ethnic groups under the control of an apparatus that, like the Liao and Jin, mixed the consensual but often bloody decision-making traditions of the steppes with the hierarchical and authoritarian approach of China. There developed under the Yuan a four-class system for allocating legal and fiscal privileges, whose basis was the degree of historical closeness a given group had to the house of Chinggis Khan and the timing of the group's addition to the empire. Thus, first in order came the Mongols, who were themselves differentiated by inherited rank. Second came other foreigners, including especially Tanguts and Turks. They were called *semu*. (Marco Polo seems to have been treated by his hero Khubilai as a *semu* and used by him as a special emissary to report on military operations in Yunnan and Burma.) Third came the "Hanren," which took in all former subjects of the Jin empire, including Chinese, Khitans, and Jurchens. Last came the "Nanren," former subjects of the Southern Song. Wealth and population were overwhelmingly concentrated at the bottom of the ethnic hierarchy, but south China's legal and political disadvantages were tacitly compensated for by its much lighter administrative and tax burden, as compared to north China.

As emperor of China, Khubilai can be credited with the accomplishment of at least two major projects—the creation of a national system of paper money backed by precious metal reserves, and the reextension of the Grand Canal north to Dadu, a portion defunct since China was last unified in the late Tang.

After Khubilai's death in 1294, the Yuan dynasty gradually evolved into a less exploitative regime that more and more focused its efforts on addressing the needs and wants of its huge Chinese population. Chinese demands for the institution of a civil service examination system based in the *daoxue* texts and doctrines of Zhu Xi were answered affirmatively by the Yuan authorities and made reality starting in 1315. Young men from all four of the officially recognized ethnic classes were invited to compete in the examinations. A quota of twenty-five *jinshi* every three years was set for each of the four. Thus, Mongol and *semu* youths, domiciled in the provinces without access to the *keshig* (the largely hereditary imperial cadet corps of fourteen thousand or so stationed in Dadu), were given the opportunity to study *daoxue*, become Chinese-style degree-holders, and enter bureaucracy in that fashion. Bureaucrats who entered government by way of hereditary privilege or clerical training always outnumbered degree-holders, even in the Tang and Song. Although never more than a tiny fraction of Yuan bureaucracy, degree-holders tended to occupy positions of low rank but high visibility in the various literary academies or in the Censorate, where their intellectual credentials and ability to articulate at times overwhelmed the great majority of their colleagues.

The forty-year period from 1294 to 1333 saw nine emperors come and go. Far from being autocrats, the later Yuan emperors were creatures of factional struggles among various alignments of Mongol and

Turkish (*semu*) grandees. By 1328, one faction went so far as to enlist the support of Confucianist degree-holding officials, many of them Chinese. By the late 1330s, there developed a split between those high elites who favored the Confucian style and those who insisted upon Mongol traditions. The Mongolists won in 1333, but lost in 1340. The 1340s featured a very different split, as a series of natural disasters demanded that the government formulate and apply remedies. One faction, consisting of officials of various ethnic classes, took the minimalist Confucian line that the disasters were best handled by giving local officials on the scene all the authority necessary to bring relief. The other faction, also polyethnic in composition, echoed the centralist, world-transforming approach of Wang Anshi.

Catastrophic floods had destroyed the north China portion of the Grand Canal, wrecked the Hejian salt works (a major source of government income), and effected a shift in the lower course of the Yellow River, so that it now entered the sea north of the Shandong peninsula instead of debouching into the Huai River system south of the peninsula as before. The energetic young Mongol chancellor Toghto argued that fixing the canal and the salt works required that the Yellow River first be rerouted to its former "natural" channel, south of the Shandong peninsula. And so, in what was the greatest hydraulic project ever undertaken in China to that point, the Yuan central government successfully engineered the rerouting of the Yellow River over the period May to December 1351.

Meanwhile, in actions that were prompted by the natural disasters, but only tangentially related to Toghto's rechanneling project, all of China erupted in an orgy of violence. Inspired and loosely directed by sectarian holy figures, first in the north from 1351, then in the south from 1352, gangs of young idlers and drifters donned red headbands and went from county seat to county seat, killing officials and rich landlords and declaring an end to Yuan rule. There had been nothing quite like this in China since the Yellow Turban revolt of 184.

The Red Turbans, as they were called, at first caught the Yuan military and police off guard and sent them reeling in shock. However, Chancellor Toghto thought suppressing these riots to be a task that lay within the competence of the central government to manage, and he had the emperor appoint him supreme director of the whole crackdown. His method was traditionally and effectively Mongol. Just as the

Mongols had earlier built Dadu and conquered south China in the 1270s, so too now suppressing the Red Turbans nationwide required commandeering both local and foreign manpower and expertise and putting these together in temporary task-oriented groupings in such a way that no generals or other leaders were ever in a position to arrogate power and authority to themselves. Toghto personally took command of a heterogeneous force whose job was to clear the route of the yet to be rebuilt Grand Canal. Thus, he recovered Xuzhou from rebel control in October 1352. Then, he turned to a costly project to convert north China's farmland into rice paddies. Late in 1354, he assembled a huge multinational force to besiege the Grand Canal city of Gaoyou. The taking of Gaoyou would have broken the back of the great riots and restored Yuan central authority nationwide.

It was not to be. Toghto had issued huge sums of unbacked paper currency to fund all of his activities, and runaway inflation was about to destroy the Yuan monetary system altogether. In his years in office, Toghto had made enemies, many of them of the conservative Confucian persuasion, who did not like the chancellor's centralizing methods. In the end, the emperor was persuaded to issue an edict dismissing him from office. Toghto received that edict in January 1355 while with his army besieging Gaoyou. Though urged not to, he obeyed the edict. The siege thereupon collapsed. The besieging army units melted away. The rebels inside Gaoyou could hardly believe their good fortune. Other rebel remnants, chased into hiding in the back country (among them the future Ming founder, Zhu Yuanzhang), found themselves with a sudden new lease on life. China was headed for thirteen more years of destructive internal warfare.

The Creation of Ming China

The Ming founding of 1368 was historically unique in several respects. The founder, Zhu Yuanzhang (1328–1398), was not at the outset a military commander, nor could he boast of a high social pedigree, or even an educated background. He came from a central China peasant family, almost all of whose members died in the diseases, famine, and wars of the 1340s and 1350s. Not even the founders of the Han in 202 BCE or the Latter Liang in 907 were burdened by origins so precariously low. A grim and suspicious autodidact, the Ming founder (posthumously named Taizu) inspired fear and respect, but no love or devotion. Yet until he accomplished the feat, no dynasty had ever built up strength in the south first, then marched north to reunify China. (All earlier attempts to do that had failed: the Eastern Jin in the fourth century, the Northern Song late in the eleventh century, and the Southern Song early in the thirteenth). And no earlier founder ever developed, and to so high a degree imposed, a visionary program aimed at a total transformation of China. Only Mao Zedong is comparable.

The Ming unification and subsequent remaking of China was only to a limited degree a product of revanchist ardor. Rather, it was the product of the cold, relentless institutional engineering that Taizu conducted from his earliest moments as leader of a contingent of former Red Turban rebels that emerged from hiding after Toghto's dismissal, migrated south across the Yangzi, and captured Nanjing in 1356. Taizu's institutional engineering was centered in a profound distrust of human nature, a belief that no one could be trusted for long with discretionary authority of any sort, that all functionaries—civil, military, or princely—always needed to have their powers checked and divided, and to be under scrutiny, both open and covert, at all times. Taizu's penal repressions were frequent and savage. There is no doubt that all this allowed, indeed required, a personal despotism.

But it was a despotism girded by a Confucian rationale. Unlike earlier dynastic founders, Ming Taizu actively sought ideological direction. By the early 1360s, he had recruited to his cause several Confucian intellectuals of national reputation from Zhejiang province, including especially Liu Ji (1311–1375) and Song Lian (1310–1381). These intellectuals, who had been thinking and writing about the future of China, impressed upon their patron a totalizing vision of national sociomoral transformation, a return to the utopian norms of Golden Age antiquity. This was their remedy for the laxity, carelessness, and corruption of Yuan rule that, in their view, allowed the Red Turban horrors to happen and caused the Yuan collapse. So, the Ming founder was advised to take up the duties not just of ruler, but also of teacher to the people of China. He was a "ruler-teacher" (*junshi*). The guiding slogan was "repossessing antiquity" (*fugu*). No founder, since the semimythical golden age itself, two millennia earlier, had assumed so much responsibility.

A burst of administrative energy was not untypical of major dynastic foundations, but the Ming was exceptionally energetic. It inherited a China battered by seventeen years of war and defenseless against whatever the Ming founder now wished to impose upon it. Teaching the people ethical fundamentals was believed to be essential to the reinstitution of order. Ming propaganda was produced and disseminated in great quantities. Reams of rules, regulations, and exhortations, written in part by the founder himself, let the people of China know what was expected of them in the way of good behavior. Resolute efforts were made to penetrate society down to the village level and even out into the fields. Blind men led by young boys went about sounding a clapper and shouting so that all the working peasants could hear Taizu's "Six Maxims" demanding good behavior. Minds everywhere had to be remolded so that the horrors of the late Yuan collapse might never be repeated. For those who declined to heed the warnings and teachings, the penalties were merciless.

For thirty years Taizu ruled China with an iron hand. His aim to remold ethically the people of China sat uneasily alongside his fundamental distrust of them. He soon grew dissatisfied with inherited institutions. He found that he could not rely on the civil service examination system to deliver honest officials, and so he scrapped it in 1373 in favor of a system of recommendations (later he restored the exams). He found he could not trust his bureaucracy, and he purged it heavily and bloodily on several occasions. He found he could not trust his prime minister, so in 1380 he abolished the office altogether, leaving the emperor himself as sole supervisor of some twelve different organs of government. He found he could not trust the generals who had conquered China for him; at first he made them a hereditary nobility, but in 1393 he destroyed them in a huge purge and assigned their high-level military responsibilities to fifteen of his sons, enfeoffed mainly in the north as regional princes.

The Ming founder's policy was deliberately aimed at maintaining national unity and order at minimal fiscal cost. The huge Ming army was made self-supporting and hereditary, which allowed tax rates on everyone else to be set very low. The people themselves were required to perform low-level judicial, police, and tax-collecting functions for free. Civil service was cut to minimal size and was not generously paid. Uninterested in empire, early Ming China confined itself to a China proper that the Yuan had enlarged to a size eight times that of present-day France.

The Ming Refounded: Jianwen (r. 1398–1402) and Yongle (r. 1402–1424)

The Ming founder's *Ancestral Instructions* mandated throne succession strictly by primogeniture. Taizu's eldest son died in 1392. Arguably, the next in line would be the next eldest son. But instead, when the founder died in 1398, the throne passed, surely on his orders, to the eldest surviving son in the next generation, his grandson, the twenty-one-year-old Jianwen emperor. In a fashion that would later become a pattern in Ming successions, the new emperor sponsored a major policy reversal. Influenced by a younger generation of Confucian intellectuals, Fang Xiaoru (1357–1402) in particular, Jianwen proceeded to reintroduce trust into social and institutional relationships, to concede much to local initiative, and to dismantle the despotic machinery of rectification that had become counterproductive. He also began to remove the armed princes, a troublesome remaining legacy of the founder's radical mistrust. All went well, until the strongest of the young successor's princely uncles, Zhu Di (Prince of Yan), was confronted at his fief in present-day Beijing. Jianwen held an overwhelming edge in manpower and resources. Victory ought to have been his. But strategic errors, acts of treachery, and bad luck fatally afflicted the imperial side. Zhu Di's forces prevailed. On July 13, 1402, the rebel prince entered Nanjing. The imperial palace was set ablaze, and no sure sign of Jianwen was ever seen again. The Ming dynasty was, in effect, refounded. Zhu Di was emperor. The reign title he chose was, inexplicably almost, Yongle, or "perpetual joy."

The Yongle reign (1402–1424) consisted less of joy than in an orgy of activity. It ranks with the reign of another usurper, Tang Taizong, as one of the most spectacular in China's long history.

On the home front, the examination system, based in Zhu Xi Neo-Confucianism, became permanently established as definitely the most prestigious avenue to office for the educated youth of the realm. To ensure standardization and Neo-Confucian orthodoxy, the Yongle emperor's government edited and issued to every school in the realm three large compendia as study guides. Also edited and published were a giant revision of the Buddhist Tripitaka and a colossal collectaneum of nearly all writing surviving in China from earliest times down to Yongle's reign. Construction having gone on for many years, a completely new city of Beijing was declared the official capital of China in 1421. The Grand Canal, rebuilt yet again, connected the city to the grain surpluses of the lower Yangzi.

Abroad, the inward focus of the Ming founder was completely reversed. Palace eunuchs were sent on diplomatic missions to the tribes of the Amur River region of northern Manchuria, to Xinjiang, and as far west as Samarkand and Herat. The purpose was to proclaim the Ming and to encourage submissions to, or at least tributary relations with, the Ming court. Agreements were made with Japan and with local authorities in Tibet and Nepal. Most extraordinary of all, of course, were the five fantastically expensive sea voyages led by the eunuch Zheng He to Southeast Asia, the Persian Gulf, and even as far as the east African coast, from 1405 until 1433.

The relocation of the Ming capital from Nanjing to Beijing signaled a shift from what might have evolved into a regime eager to foster economic growth like the Song to a more warlike regime like the Han or Tang, whose main preoccupation was military security. Beijing was a garrison city. The Mongol court, so recently expelled from China, was perceived to be the principal enemy. Yongle's relations with the Mongols were exceedingly hostile. His father, Taizu, had believed that the Mongol court was unreconciled to its loss of China, and in a series of assaults into the steppes culminating in 1388 he all but destroyed the Yuan court in exile. Yongle as prince participated personally in much of this military activity. Later, as emperor, he faced two new and competing Mongol confederations: the Oyirads in the west and Arughtai's people in the east. Yongle's strategy was to protect China from their raids by supporting whichever confederation was the weaker at any given moment. He personally led four military expeditions into the steppes: 1410 (against Arughtai), 1414 (against the

Oyirads), 1423 (against Arughtai), and 1424 (also against Arughtai). Yongle died on August 12, 1424, perhaps of elixir poisoning, while returning from the last one. No Chinese emperor had ever before personally commanded war expeditions into Mongolia. Yongle's doing so contributed little to China's security in the long run. Perhaps for reasons of economy, he pulled his forward defense posts southward, out of the steppe margins. He also declined to subsidize Mongolia, as the Yuan dynasty had done. For as long as the Ming lasted, a legacy of violence and bad planning regularly vitiated efforts to achieve a peaceful resolution of differences. (From 1472, the Ming began building what Europeans later called the Great Wall of China, arguably a fallback measure that signaled the failure of all better policy alternatives. Portions of such a wall had been built in early times, but what the Ming built was a wholly new construction.)

There was also the curious Vietnam invasion of 1406, an action that was not very bound up with China's perceived security needs. Ming China under Yongle was asserting a global moral hegemony, arrogating to itself the authority to confer recognition on foreign rulers, but also accepting an obligation to intervene forcefully, when called upon, on those rulers' behalf. Zheng He's fleet intervened in civil war in Java and issued threats elsewhere, in support of rulers granted recognition by the Ming, but under challenge from internal rebels. This was also the case in Vietnam, where the deposed Trần ruling house appealed to the Ming court to help restore it to power. The 1406 invasion was a success, but the Trần were in no condition to resume their rule. The Yongle emperor then made an ill-advised decision to annex Vietnam outright as a province of China. The consequences were unpleasant. Yongle soon lost interest; Vietnam was wretchedly administered; and rebellions against Ming rule were unrelenting. In 1427, after Yongle's death, the Ming decided to swallow its pride, withdraw, and officially recognize the Latter Lê dynasty as the legitimate rulers of the country.

The Middle Years of the Ming

Yongle's eldest son and successor, the Hongxi emperor, was on the verge of reversing many of Yongle's policies and moving the capital back to Nanjing when he died in 1425 at the age of forty-six, after a reign of barely eight months. His own eldest son, the Xuande emperor, aged twenty-six, kept the capital at Beijing, but he reversed many other policies of Yongle (the maritime expeditions, the Vietnam annexation) and ruled until his own death in 1435. These rulers—Yongle, Hongxi, and Xuande—all had administrative experience before coming to power, were personally involved in governance, and together saw Ming China come to something of a pinnacle of power and prestige. After 1435, things changed. Emperors were badly schooled, often came to power as children, and their later involvement in administration tended to be intermittent or capricious. Xuande's elder son and successor came to the throne as the Zhengtong emperor at the age of nine in 1435. In 1449, he was persuaded by his eunuchs to command in person a military expedition into the steppes, where unfortunately he was ambushed, captured, and held hostage by Esen, khan of the Oyirad Mongols. The atmosphere in Beijing turned frantic as high officials debated whether to evacuate north China altogether. Minister of War Yu Qian was most forceful, and his opinion carried the day—to depose Zhengtong in absentia, ignore his baby son, and enthrone his older half brother, aged twenty-one, as the Jingtai emperor. That act deprived Zhengtong of all further value, and Esen returned his now useless hostage to Beijing in 1450. The deposed emperor was put under house arrest. In 1457, however, he returned to power (as the Tianshun emperor) when a coup on his behalf put an end to the life of his brother. (Another anomaly in the imperial succession took place in 1521, when the Zhengde emperor died childless at the age of thirty, and, again, it was high officials who decided that his successor should be a cousin of the same generation, the fourteen-year-old Prince of Xing, who ruled as the Jiajing emperor, from 1521 to 1567.)

As these later Ming emperors came to show a lack of interest, or competence, in governing the realm, there arose a sort of free-floating authority that became a bone of contention among palace eunuchs, officials of the Censorate and offices of scrutiny, and the grand secretaries (constitutionally improvised successors to the prime ministerial function that was eliminated in 1380; the grand secretaries were advisers only, but occasionally they reached for executive authority as well). Partisan organization among bureaucrats was a statutory crime, but during the sixteenth century there developed in the bureaucracy informal but wide-ranging networks often inspired by ideas of moral rededication and Confucian renewal. The networks heavily influenced education, examination criteria, and official personnel placement. Members at times became vehement critics of government.

Wang Yangming (1472–1529) and his many ardent followers challenged the official Zhu Xi orthodoxy. Wang's career was that of a highly effective provincial official. His doctrines stressed ethical self-realization and interpersonal ethical activism. His powerfully attractive reinterpretation of the Confucian way bypassed such standing institutions as the national school system and, rather like Zhu Xi's original *daoxue* movement in the Southern Song, was propagated mainly in informal discussion circles and in privately funded academies. The movement was less confrontational than Zhu's. Still, from 1570 to 1579, long after Wang's death, the reforming Grand Secretary Zhang Juzheng (1525–1582) closed down all the academies for criticizing national policy, wasting resources, and distracting officials and students from their proper duties. That action effectively put an end to the prevalence of Wang Yangming studies in China (his doctrines would later find welcome soil in Japan). Zhu Xi orthodoxy then underwent a major revival, but not under official auspices. Ironically, it was revived in private discussion circles (attended by off-duty officials and students) and in private academies, including especially the famous Donglin Academy in Wuxi (Jiangsu province), founded in 1604. The Donglin doctrines were aimed not inwardly, as Wang's had been, but outwardly, and strove to bring about the complete ethical cleansing and remaking of Ming government. But that is to jump ahead of the story.

The Reign of Jiajing
1522–1566

The forty-four years of the Jiajing emperor's reign, coming as it did late in the middle of the Ming, is as good a moment as any to gauge the often paradoxical qualities of the mature imperial Chinese institutional system.

A teenage prince living far to the south in Hubei province, Jiajing was called to the throne in 1522 by Chief Grand Secretary Yang Tinghe, de facto dictator of China upon the death of the childless Zhengde emperor, the young prince's cousin. Immediately there developed a profound struggle between Jiajing and Yang's faction in the Grand Secretariat and Hanlin Academy over the highly technical and deceptively trivial question of whether Jiajing should posthumously promote his deceased princely father to the status of emperor, or whether he should, in effect, disown his own father and accept Zhengde's father, the Hongzhi emperor (r. 1488–1505), as his adopted father. This was the so-called Great Rites Controversy, which stretched over many years, ending only in 1545 with Jiajing's triumphal emplacement of his father's spirit tablet in the imperial ancestral temple. Jiajing won every earlier round in the battle, including especially the great showdown of 1524, when over two hundred high-ranking central officials conducted a mass protest in front of the Forbidden City, demanding that Jiajing agree to make himself Hongzhi's son by adoption and so maintain the integrity of an unbroken Ming imperial descent line. The demonstrators were utterly serious and totally sincere. They knew very well they were risking their careers and probably their lives as well. But in their view, the issue went to the very heart of China's civilization. The demands of public imperial ritual had to trump the young emperor's personal and selfish concern for private family ritual. Otherwise, all of China would imitate Jiajing's selfishness and collapse in an orgy of hedonism.

Jiajing resolutely faced this demonstration down. He ordered the arrest and cruel flogging of the demonstrators. Seventeen men died of the beating. In 1528, Jiajing ordered published an official text that authoritatively stated his own side of the issue. To the end of the Ming, his position was never again challenged. Yet in a way, the demonstrators were right: Jiajing's stance did affect family order nationwide. It seems to have opened the floodgates that had long held back pressures to expand the family system. Orthodox Neo-Confucianism, in its official Zhu Xi version as sanctioned by the Ming state, did not permit limitless lineage expansion. But Jiajing's victory in the Great Rites Controversy was a victory of personal feeling over text-based literalism and rigidity. By and large, the people of China were on Jiajing's side. As will be noted later, the formation of large endowed lineages with ancestral halls proceeded apace over the course of the sixteenth century. But here lay an unexpected paradox: Wang Yangming and his philosophical followers in bureaucracy sided with Jiajing; it was Zhu Xi adherents who opposed him. Yet Jiajing disdained Wang and his school. The rites issue notwithstanding, the Zhu Xi orthodoxy continued to enjoy the emperor's support. Jiajing was no revolutionary by intention.

Nor was he a loved and admired leader of his realm. He tolerated no criticism. He categorically distrusted high officials and subjected many of them to terribly brutal treatment. Several attempts were made on his life, none so telling, perhaps, as his palace ladies' near success at killing him by strangulation in 1542. From that point, Jiajing moved out of the Forbidden City to a detached palace in a nearby imperial park, where he occupied himself with Daoist adepts and slowly (and accidentally) poisoned himself with their elixirs of immortality. Legal and personnel matters he often decided by consulting the spirits with a planchette. Bouts of depression alternated with fits of rage.

During Jiajing's long reign, the dynasty temporarily lost control of both its northern and its eastern (coastal) borders. The Mongols demanded the opening of trade relations, and when Jiajing refused, they conducted devastating raids deep into Ming territory. From the 1540s, Japanese traders and their coastal Chinese partners (including members of powerful local lineages) likewise turned to horrific plundering expeditions inland when Jiajing denied their trade demands. The Portuguese tried to open foreign trade as early as the 1520s but were flatly denied. Jiajing clung steadfastly to an unimaginative policy of unrelenting hostility against pressures from both outside and inside Ming China to liberalize economic relations with the rest of the world.

The emperor was fortunate that none of his enemies sought to challenge the legitimacy of Ming rule. The Mongols wanted trade relations only and harbored no plans to conquer China again. The traders and pirates of the coastal regions built large fleets and fortified bases onshore, but they developed no dynastic ambitions. High officials and their factions competed over the question of how best to satisfy Jiajing's foreign policy demands. Chief Grand Secretary Xia Yan's idea was to take on the Mongols aggressively, chiefly by invading and annexing the Ordos desert region, which was Altan Khan's main staging area for raids. That idea failed for logistic and other reasons, and Xia was executed in 1548. His rival and successor, Yan Song, preferred wall building and a passive defense, but this failed to stop Mongol raiding; Jiajing, who never wholly trusted Yan, reduced him to commoner status in 1565, confiscating his possessions, and executing his son, mainly on corruption charges lodged by Yan's bureaucratic enemies. Similarly, a campaign of extreme violence against the coastal traders and pirates during the years from 1547 to 1550 backfired and had to be dropped. A subsequent policy of coaxing surrenders worked rather better. A military genius, Qi Jiguang, who enjoyed the protection of high officials in Beijing, organized effective antipirate defenses in the 1560s. Unknown to Jiajing, it was regional officials who ceded Macao to the Portuguese as a permanent trading base in the 1550s. Then, upon Jiajing's death on January 23, 1567, the Ming government rescinded the ban on private maritime trade and opened peaceful tribute and trade relations with Altan Khan's Mongols.

The Jiajing reign illustrates the overall strength and resiliency of the Ming system. Forty-four years of a misguided foreign policy, and forty-four years of internal military revolts, famines, and revenue shortfalls under an arguably dysfunctional emperor, would have been more than enough to cause the collapse of one of China's top-heavy dynasties of the sixth century. A thousand years later, the sixteenth-century Ming, for all its inadequacies, was never in danger of falling. Its legitimacy went without serious challenge. Beneath the turbulence of high politics, routine administration continued as ever. Despite trade bans, foreign (Japanese and American) silver poured into the country in payment for Ming silk and porcelain. People on their own undertook to organize large and powerful lineages. They took control of local education. The Ming state either ignored all this or could do little about it.

Late Ming Foreign Relations

Zhang Juzheng was chief grand secretary during the minority of the Wanli emperor (r. 1572–1620), a child of nine at accession. Zhang was a practical reformer, not a visionary. By ruthlessly cutting expenditures, he accumulated very large silver reserves. He patronized a team of talented officials: Wang Chonggu (who negotiated a peace agreement with Altan Khan of the Tümet Mongols); Pan Jixun (who engineered a reconfiguration of the lower reaches of the Yellow River); and Qi Jiguang (who trained and led effective defense forces against pirates along the coast and Mongols to the north). Zhang's nationwide land tax reform was cut short by his untimely death in office. His arrogance and harsh repression of critics ensured his posthumous condemnation and the undoing of most of his reforms.

Ming China lasted 276 years. During that long era of unified imperial rule, China's population may have tripled to nearly two hundred million, with at least a commensurate quantitative growth in the national economy—less centered on large urban nodes as in the Song, but quasi-rural, decentralized, and heavily competitive. The Ming state was too understaffed to be able to tax this growth effectively, nor, as rising quantities of silver bullion from Japan and South America entered the country through illegal trade channels during the sixteenth century, could it control the national monetary supply—as the Song state had been able to do half a millennium earlier. What did happen was that local officials made piecemeal adjustments to the increasing availability of bulk silver, and gradually the dynasty's whole fiscal base shifted from labor services and taxes in kind to a simplified lump-sum silver payment. China exported over three million pieces of Jingdezhen porcelain westward to Europe, mainly in Dutch ships, between 1602 and 1657. Ming silk and porcelain went eastward too, in return for silver, after the establishment of the Spanish galleon routes from Manila to Acapulco in 1564 and 1565. It has been argued that Ming China was probably not an outpost, but the central focus of an emerging global economy. It has also been argued that price inflation in China brought on by the uncontrolled influx of foreign silver helped occasion the collapse of the Ming in the 1640s.

Ming China's posture in the larger world of its time was, thus, riddled with contradictions. Foreign relations theory gave China pride of place as the ethical center and moral arbiter of the universe, symbolized in the so-called tribute system, with its extremely strict controls on all relations with foreign states and foreigners. It was never possible to bring Japan comfortably into this system, and so all official links with it were cut in 1549. That helped boost predatory Japanese piracy along the China coast. Despite official interdicts on private foreign trade, there grew during the course of the Ming an international maritime community, featuring Japanese, Dutch, Spanish, Portuguese, as well as Chinese sea traders and rovers, and a trading network extending from the coast of China to Japan, Southeast Asia, and from there to Europe and the Americas. Likewise with the Mongols: the Ming was seldom able to do better than to encourage tribal anarchy, but anarchy encouraged continued Mongol raiding along the increasingly walled frontier. The frontier area was one of great intermixing, with many Chinese peasants illegally settled in Mongol territory under Mongol protection; large numbers of Mongols, many of them soldiers in Ming service, settled inside China; and Ming border troops carrying on a lively trade in contraband with the enemy.

The Ming made some grudging exceptions to the official tributary model, partially lifting the ban on private trade and quietly granting a trading base to the Portuguese at Macao in 1557. In 1583, the Jesuit missionary Matteo Ricci (1552–1610) was given permission to live in China, and in 1598 he was allowed to move to Beijing. The Jesuits, despite their small numbers, made many thousands of converts in the late Ming, and not just among the educated elite. In Beijing, they had good success introducing mathematical cartography, Euclidean geometry, calendrical astronomy, mining technology, and advanced gunpowder weaponry to the Ming government. (There was a parallel burst of interest among the late Ming literati in Chinese technologies, including especially agriculture, and in a dispassionate and thorough review of all problems of national administration). Jesuit books and annual letters, describing the fall of the Ming dynasty and the rise of the Qing, brought current events in East Asia to public attention in Europe for the first time.

The Late Ming: Internal Developments

While late Ming China developed economic, cultural, and technological ties to the outside world to a degree perhaps not seen since Tang China's links to Central Asia, Iran, India, and Buddhism nearly a millennium earlier, those ties, though significant, did not override in importance developments specific to China and East Asia. Earlier under the tutelage of Zhang Juzheng, the Wanli emperor, as he came of age, became interested in military affairs. The civil bureaucracy would have none of it. So, Wanli simply ignored the bureaucracy and developed a parallel system—a corps of eunuch tax collectors and supervisors of mines whose job was to provide revenues sufficient (when combined with the savings amassed by Zhang) to fund war making. This made possible several large campaigns, including especially Wanli's military interventions against the Japanese in Korea in 1593 and 1597, operations that enjoyed some success and ended when the Japanese leader Hideyoshi died in 1598 and the Japanese withdrew. In 1619, a special nationwide tax surcharge was imposed to finance a major punitive expedition into Manchuria to dispose of a pugnacious Jurchen leader named Nurhaci. This time, despite Ming superiority in numbers and in advanced European firearms, the expedition was poorly planned and badly led and was never able to use its accustomed siege tactics; the Ming armies were decisively routed by Nurhaci in a series of open-field encounters.

The summer of 1620 witnessed the death of Wanli, the accession and sudden death of his son and successor, the Taichang emperor, and then the succession of Wanli's fourteen-year-old grandson, the disastrous Tianqi emperor (r. 1620–1627). Rather like the Hongxi emperor in his short reign in 1424, Taichang sponsored a major policy reversal during his single month of rule in the summer of 1620, putting an end to militarism and eunuch paragovernment and restoring to primacy the civil bureaucracy, now dominated by the moralizing Donglin faction. Under Tianqi, policy shifted back again. In 1624, the Donglin party staged an all-out protest. Led by palace eunuch Wei Zhongxian, the anti-Donglin officials in the bureaucracy and central police arrested and tortured to death some thirteen leading lights in the Donglin faction and purged hundreds of others from office. Meanwhile, the Jurchen khan Nurhaci inflicted another ugly defeat on Ming forces in Manchuria. But in 1626, under the aegis of Wei Zhongxian, the Ming defenders of the city of Ningyuan, thanks in large part to the accurate fire of their Portuguese cannon, at last put Nurhaci to rout. Nurhaci died later that same year. For a brief moment, things looked promising for the Ming.

However, Tianqi died without an heir in 1627 (his five children had all died in infancy). He named and was succeeded by his younger half brother, the Chongzhen emperor, aged sixteen. Chongzhen was conscientious. He sponsored yet another top-level policy shift. Wei Zhongxian and his adherents were purged. Wei committed suicide. But so degraded had political life become as a result of the extreme violence provoked by the Donglin, and so unremitting the thirst for revenge, that the petulant Chongzhen, conscientious as he may have been, could never harness the bureaucracy effectively and get it to face the grave problems that now threatened the realm on all sides. Meanwhile, the Confucian moralists regrouped as the "Restoration Society" (*Fu she*), a nationwide league of discussion groups that argued, much as the Donglin had done, that a national spiritual awakening and renewal must precede any practical reform effort.

The Ming Collapse

The Chongzhen reign (1627–1644), the last of an intact Ming dynasty, was not a happy time. A corrupt provincial and local bureaucracy; a monetary system in which the state repeatedly debased the copper coinage; and subsistence crises in many parts of the country, but especially in north China—these factors helped prompt widespread banditry that, with the rise of Li Zicheng and Zhang Xianzhong in Shaanxi from 1628, began to assume threatening proportions. Li and Zhang were two among many military deserters from the northern frontier who gathered distressed peasant youths and began mobile raiding operations, first in Shaanxi, and soon spreading elsewhere. If these uprisings were the only problem facing the Ming court, they could have been managed. A civil official, Hong Chengchou, in charge of military operations, inflicted a series of severe defeats on Li and by 1638 had all but captured him. But then Hong was transferred to the Manchurian front, where, by 1639, Nurhaci's successor Hung Taiji had renamed his people the Manchus, declared a Chinese-style Qing dynasty, subdued Korea, and absorbed the eastern Mongols. He became patron of the Dalai Lama and the Yellow Hat sect of Tibetan Buddhism, welcomed Chinese civil and military defectors (including Hong himself in 1642), and made several deep raids into Ming territory. Thanks largely to this Manchu activity, Li gained a reprieve. A horrible drought in Henan in 1639 and 1640 prompted Li's reemergence in that province, where he raised havoc, conquered walled towns, and was conducting a long siege of Kaifeng in 1642 when a catastrophic flood of the Yellow River, fed by heavy rains, completely destroyed the city. Li withdrew west to Shaanxi in 1643, where (shades of Huang Chao in 881) he declared a dynasty, conducted civil service examinations, and at last made a serious attempt to shift from banditry to orderly administration in a bid to succeed the Ming. A well-executed two-pronged military assault seized Beijing on April 25, 1644, with a minimum of disorder. Rather than negotiate an abdication, the Chongzhen emperor hanged himself. Nominally, Li's Shun dynasty now ruled China, but only for forty days—in early June it collapsed.

The Shun did show some populist features. Rather than tax the poor, the Shun regime funded itself by plundering the rich. Li's men seized the imperial Ming treasury. They forced imperial princes and in-laws to disgorge huge sums. They crudely graded eunuchs, merchants, great landlords, and high officials by income level and took some 20 percent to 30 percent of their riches. The Shun dynasty, within weeks, is reckoned to have collected some seventy million taels of silver altogether. The regime revived Tang official nomenclature. Positive references were made to the early Tang equal field system. Much of north China accepted Shun-appointed magistrates. Many officials and literati deserted the Ming cause and accepted the Shun. As emperor, the ex-bandit Li lived modestly and seemed to want to rule responsibly. What, then, went wrong? Why did the Shun not succeed as successor to the Ming?

There were two sets of difficulties, one internal to the Shun, the other relating to Li's relationships to external forces and their leaders. Internally, Li's military elite, of bandit origin like himself, was loath to accept civilian control. Very shortly after their orderly entry into Beijing, they cast off all restraint to engage in arbitrary arrests, torture, murder, and looting. Externally, there were too many failed negotiations, stemming from Li's visceral dislike for defectors. In 1641, for example, Li did not take advantage of an opportunity to bring aboard fellow rebel Zhang and his forces. In February 1644, while Li and his army were still on the march to Beijing, he received but ignored a letter from the Manchu regent Dorgon proposing joint operations. In April and May, Li fumbled away any hope of joining forces with Wu Sangui, the leading Ming commander still serving on the Manchurian frontier. Wu's family, living in Beijing, had been mistreated by Li's men. Wu's father was made a hostage. In May 1644, Wu proposed and Dorgon agreed to join forces against Li's attack on Wu's position. Li's army, gorged with Beijing loot, seemed to lack interest in the fight. It was routed. The Shun collapse was immediate and catastrophic. The joined forces of Dorgon and Wu entered Beijing on June 6, 1644. The Shun fled in disarray back to Shaanxi. Sometime in 1645, Li disappeared, at the approximate age of thirty-nine. He was never seen again. The Manchu conquest of China had begun. Like the Mongol conquest four centuries earlier, the Manchu takeover would take half a century to complete.

Qing China: The Founding from 1644

The Manchu Qing conquest machine featured so many weaknesses that, far from being inevitable, its eventual success seems hard to account for. Among these weaknesses was the poverty of their Manchurian base; the perennial outsider's problem of reconciling tribal tradition with Chinese institutional norms; frictions among Chinese, Manchu, and Mongol ethnic groups; and murderous rivalries among the members of the ruling Aisin Gioro clan. These weaknesses would be enough to explain a Qing failure, had it occurred. But of course, the Qing in the end created the largest of all the China-centered empires, larger than even the Yuan or the Tang. And the Qing dynasty, from its declaration in 1639, somehow survived every kind of challenge until finally it abdicated to Yuan Shikai on February 12, 1912.

The nominal founding emperor of the Qing dynasty in China, known by the reign title Shunzhi (r. 1643–1661), was only six years old in 1644 when the Qing forces took Beijing. He suffered from what appears to have been tuberculosis and died in 1661 at the young age of twenty-three. Although volatile in temperament, he was also exceptionally studious and a committed devotee of Chan Buddhism—traits perhaps more to be expected in a sovereign of a mature or failing dynasty than in the ruler of a rising one. But while he lived, Shunzhi ruled with vigor. He seized control of the reins of state not long after the the death of the dictatorial prince-regent Dorgon in 1650. He then went so far as to reformulate Manchu policy and restyle its institutions in a pro-Chinese direction and to sponsor severe crackdowns on bureaucratic corruption and factionalism. Shunzhi was succeeded by another minor, his seven-year-old son Kangxi (r. 1661–1722). But Kangxi and the next four emperors, who ruled into the middle of the nineteenth century, were each blessed with long or very long reigns, and each showed an active interest in administration. On balance, their successes outweighed their many mistakes and failings. Securing good rulers was in large part a product of a Qing innovation: instead of Ming-style automatic primogeniture, with not even regencies permitted for child emperors, Qing rulers secretly chose their successors from among their many eligible sons. Not even the heir apparent knew who the choice was until his father's death, when the successor's name was at last revealed.

Key to the success of the early Qing enterprise was the Manchus' creative construction or reconstruction of Mongol and Chinese military and political institutions and the all-inclusive patronage they accorded to religious and intellectual traditions of various kinds. From very early on, the Manchus adopted the alphabetic script and the military organization of their Mongol neighbors, intermarried with the leading eastern Mongol clans, and absorbed Mongol fighters into their emerging conquest machine. Also from early on, while still confined to Manchuria, they absorbed local Chinese fighters and administrators and encouraged defections from the Ming side, especially by frontier generals such as Hong Chengchou, together with their armies. Without the Manchus' welcoming of Hong and other defectors, the coming Qing conquest of China would have been impossible. Also, starting from the 1637 visit of the fifth Dalai Lama to Mukden (Shenyang, the Manchurian capital), the Qing rulers were taken into the Yellow Hat Buddhist pantheon as incarnations of the bodhisattva Mañjuśrī, that is, as living objects of worship, and this went far to make the later Qing conquests of Mongolia and Tibet acceptable to the faithful of those vast regions. (The emperors themselves, however, remained patrons, not converts; and they made no attempt to convert the Manchu people, who were encouraged to stay with their inherited shamanic religious traditions.) The Jesuits, meanwhile, purveyed the arts and technologies of contemporary Europe to the Manchu rulers, who were eager to make use of them in the interest of empire building. These included gunnery, cartography, calendrical astronomy, and even the diplomatic skills that were used at the negotiation of the 1689 Nerchinsk agreement with Russia. And, once permanently based inside China after 1644, the Manchu rulers had to place themselves and their government convincingly into the formidable historical, institutional, and literary framework bequeathed to them by the civilization of China.

The Conquest of South China

The Qing conquest of south China was accomplished with the indispensable help of Chinese armies commanded by the turncoat Ming generals Wu Sangui (1612–1678), Geng Jingzhong (executed 1682), and Shang Kexi (d. 1676). These so-called Three Feudatories were granted a wide share of autonomy as reward for their successful assault on the Southern Ming (established at Nanjing in June 1644 and chased from there a year later, with several courts in flight until the demise of the last of them in Burma in 1659, its desperate conversion to Christianity and its plea for help from Pope Innocent X in Rome notwithstanding). Then in 1673, the Kangxi emperor made the rash decision not only to accept the aged Shang's request to retire, but also to try to abolish his Guangdong-based princedom. Afraid of becoming the next targets, Wu and Geng, based in southwestern China and in Fujian, respectively, decided to rebel. Eight years of civil war followed. Geng surrendered in 1676. Shang's son surrendered in 1677, then rebelled, but was captured and forced to commit suicide in 1680. The strongest feudatory, Wu, declared his own Zhou dynasty late in 1673 and commenced a military reconquest of China that came very close to success, but Wu died of illness in 1678. Qing forces besieged and finally destroyed his grandson and successor in Yunnan in 1681. The Kangxi emperor's victory over the feudatories had less to do with military superiority than with political skill, especially the coaxing and handling of defections from the rebel side.

Why did the so-called Southern Ming not regroup like the Eastern Jin (318–420) or the Southern Song (1127–1279) and create a new regime, stable but reduced in size, in south China? Or follow Ming Taizu's example and build power by organizing the intellectuals, officials, bandits, sectarians, rioters, local militias, and all the other detritus of dynastic collapse? Whereas Eastern Jin governance is known only dimly, it is clear that the founding of the dynasty involved mass immigration from the north, semi-independent warlords, very few bureaucrats, a reasonably competent founding emperor in Sima Rui, and a general consensus that the reconquest of the north was the regime's main and overriding purpose (as it was for Chiang Kai-shek's nationalists on Taiwan). Parts of the Eastern Jin profile fit the Southern Song as well. Even though the Qing and Southern Ming forces seldom came directly to blows, the Southern Ming, like its Jin and Song predecessors, had to rebuild institutions completely and deal somehow with semiautonomous armies, despite a shortage of officials capable of managing the task. Where the Southern Ming faltered was in badly handling not just a few things, but almost everything. There were not one but five rivalrous Southern Ming courts. All the Ming princes who would be emperors were incompetent and deeply unpopular. Lethal hatreds among the high officials, and an inability of any of the five courts to make common cause with roving armies, doomed the whole enterprise. The Eastern Jin lasted a century; the Southern Song lasted a century and a half; the so-called Southern Ming barely survived for eighteen years. But it could pride itself on its ethical posture: the Southern Ming boasted thousands of anti-Qing suicides and willing martyrs, men and women, officials and common people, far beyond the Wen Tianxiang affair of the late Southern Song, far beyond anything known to history thus far.

The leading nominal defender of the Southern Ming cause was the Zheng family, who for four generations raided Qing-held territory from their fleets and fortresses, located principally along the Fujian coast. Theirs was not the traditional continental power. The Zheng family's power was based, rather, in the greater East Asian maritime world, centered on the China coast, with lucrative trade links to Japan, Macao, the Philippines, and Southeast Asia, and connections and rivalries with such competitors as the Japanese, Portuguese, Spanish, Dutch, and others. The most famous of the Zhengs, Zheng Chenggong

(Koxinga, 1624–1662), whose Fujianese father was a Christian convert, was actually born near Nagasaki of a Japanese mother. Koxinga was able to gather huge fleets and very large fighting forces. Although he had once been a Confucian student, attending the national college in Nanjing in 1645, he never courted the literati, nor was he ever influenced in any important way by the traditional Confucian moral and political teachings. (His openly hostile relationship with his father, who defected to the Qing in 1646, was un-Confucian in the extreme.) Koxinga's power base was, by choice, commercial and military. His loyalism on behalf of the Southern Ming was for a remote cause that could in no way interfere with his freedom of action. The eventual failure of the Zheng phenomenon has roots in effective Qing countermeasures; in a downturn in the international maritime economy; and in Koxinga's own cruel and occasionally crazed behavior (and untimely death at the age of thirty-seven). The Qing was able to bring about key defections from the Zheng regime, particularly that of Admiral Shi Lang in 1646. Then during the 1660s, the Qing authorities forced the evacuation ten or so miles inland of the entire southeastern coastal population, creating a dead zone, thus depriving Koxinga of food and other resources. The Qing thwarted Koxinga's 1659 attack on Nanjing; and so he and his fleet withdrew to Taiwan, where in 1660 he compelled the Dutch to yield to him. In 1683, Shi invaded Taiwan on Qing behalf and finally put an end to the Zheng enterprise. The Kangxi emperor treated the last Zheng chieftain well. Taiwan he considered an insignificant acquisition, a useless little "ball of mud." Thus as things turned out, neither Fujian nor Taiwan would harbor any independent maritime power, any Venice. Both ended up wholly swallowed into the Qing-administered continental system.

Beyond China: Building the Qing Empire

As soon as the China domain was cleared of all serious competition (1683), the Kangxi emperor directed his attention to establishing the Qing as the dominant power in greater East and Central Asia. The Qing was not simply a Chinese-style dynasty. From the time of Nurhaci, it was also an Inner Asian khanate, with a different, mainly non-Chinese repertoire of policies and a different set of military, political, and religious institutions. In this respect, it bore resemblances to the Liao and Yuan.

The Amur River region of outer Manchuria, thinly settled by hunting and fishing tribes speaking Tungus dialects distantly akin to Manchu, had since the 1640s attracted increasing numbers of Russian Cossack pioneers eager to impose *iasak* (demands for sable and other furs) on the natives and build forts and settlements for themselves. Qing military intervention was sporadic, until, in a triumph of superior numbers, artillery, and well-organized logistics, the Cossacks were driven out by 1686. With the help of Jesuit negotiators, the famous and far-reaching Treaty of Nerchinsk was drawn up in 1689, which delimited clearly the frontier between the Qing and the Romanov empires in the Far East, established mutual security that lasted until the 1860s, and was the first step in a truly grand strategy in which the expanding Qing and Russian empires agreed to maintain peaceful relations and not use Mongols or other Inner Asian tribes against each other. (In 1727, Russia and China signed a similar agreement delimiting the Mongolia-Siberia frontier.)

Kangxi next directed his attention to the Zunghar Mongols, based in the Ili valley south of Lake Balkhash, where Galdan was building a khanate (devoted—as was the Qing—to Yellow Hat Buddhism) and aiming to annex Outer Mongolia, thus challenging the Qing for supremacy all across Inner Asia. In a series of battles fought in the steppes, two of them commanded by Kangxi in person, the Qing by 1697 forced the Zunghars back west to the Ili. In 1720, two Qing armies entered Tibet and Lhasa, ended the Zunghar occupation there, and installed Kangxi's candidate as the seventh Dalai Lama, thus making the Qing court the defender and protector of the Yellow Hats, a step that in time would go far to cement Qing power in Buddhist Inner Asia.

An exceptionally vigorous monarch, Kangxi was a contemporary of two other active rulers: Peter the Great (r. 1689–1725) and Louis XIV (r. 1664–1715). Aside from Inner Asia, Kangxi also managed to pay close attention to China. He made six inspection tours down the Grand Canal to south China. As though to surpass the Ming founder's Six Maxims, he published in 1670 sixteen moral maxims to be read out periodically to the common people of China. He sponsored large literary projects. He patronized the arts. He interested himself in the Western sciences as propagated by the Jesuits. He kept Manchu traditions alive by taking part in seasonal hunts. He ruled as autocrat for fifty-five years and died in 1722 at the age of sixty-eight. In a disputed but probably legitimate succession, his fourth son followed him and ruled as the Yongzheng emperor.

Refocusing on China: Yongzheng r. 1722–1735

During Yongzheng's reign, the Zunghars slowed the pace of Qing expansion in Inner Asia (in 1738, a Qing-Zunghar boundary agreement was reached). Yongzheng devoted most of his attention to China proper, developing a system of secret memorials through which he bypassed the regular channels of official communication and imposed his own personal scrutiny and detailed control over fiscal and personnel matters. Rather in the style of the Ming founder, Yongzheng distrusted the degree-holding elite and insisted upon a tight centralism under his own personal guidance. Through this means, he almost single-handedly conducted complex tax and fiscal reforms and developed state-managed grain storage as part of a national system of famine insurance, surely one of the most significant acts of state intervention in the economy since the days of Wang Anshi in the Northern Song, seven centuries earlier.

Yongzheng died suddenly at the age of fifty-six, possibly of elixir poisoning. His heir, secretly designated as such early on, became perhaps the most powerful ruler in the whole history of China—Yongzheng's fourth son, Hungli, aged twenty-four, who would rule for most of the eighteenth century as the Qianlong emperor (r. 1735–1799). In a way, it is appropriate that he was a contemporary of such enlightened European despots as Catherine II the Great (r. 1762–1796), Frederick II the Great (r. 1740–1786), and Maria Theresa (r. 1740–1780). Like them, Qianlong played many roles: in his case, autocrat, investigator, generalissimo, art collector, litterateur, traveler, Confucian moralist, Manchu traditionalist, historian, and holy man.

The Reign of Qianlong
1735–1799

The long and copiously documented reign of Qianlong can be divided into two nearly equal halves. The first half ended with the extermination of the last steppe empire, that of the Zunghars, in 1757, and the annexation of Eastern Turkestan (Xinjiang) in 1765. At that point, a tacit but momentous decision was taken to expand the Qing realm no further into Inner Asia. A century-long mission was accomplished: eastern Inner Asia was wholly pacified with the incorporation of Manchuria, Mongolia, Xinjiang, and Tibet, and security for China all along the troublesome northern frontiers was achieved. No big collective goal remained undone. And so into the second half of the Qianlong reign there gradually crept sloth, corruption, aimlessness, and demoralization. The once-predominating ruler allowed extraordinary powers to gather into the hands of a personal favorite, the smooth and spectacularly corrupt Manchu guardsman Hešen. Suspicious of nearly everyone besides Hešen, Qianlong still unpredictably intervened from time to time in affairs, such as in the notorious national witch hunt, the soul-stealing case of 1768.

Until about 1765, an argument can be made for considering the Qing a member in good standing of a company of expanding Eurasian empires—the Russian and perhaps even the British included. The Qing possessed the latest in gunpowder weaponry, mapmaking, diplomatic techniques, and statistics collection. Central command, communications, and logistics were already sophisticated when Qianlong set up the machinery for the so-called Grand Council in 1736. The Grand Council was a kind of extrastatutory supergovernment laid atop the regular bureaucracy, featuring its own personnel, archives, research groups, rapid communications networks, and effective modes of command and control. Thanks largely to the work of the Grand Council, Qianlong overcame a logistics breakdown that, in Yongzheng's time, contributed to the Qing stalemate with the Zunghars. It now became possible to tap the grain and other resources of China proper to support commerce, colonization, and military provisioning deep into Inner Asia. It was in Qianlong's time that the Qing became the largest of all the China-based empires (the People's Republic is some 20 percent smaller). But from 1775, because the Grand Council fell under Hešen's control (until 1799), it could do nothing to stop the horrendous corruption, the profligate costs, and the dubious results of China's late eighteenth-century wars along the western and southern frontiers.

Yet even in decline, Qing central authority continued to exert significant powers. It still tried to manage the national food supply, albeit with decreasing effectiveness. It still managed the national hydraulic system of dykes, channels, and polders along the disaster-prone Hai, Yellow, Huai, and Yangzi river basins. From 1824 to 1826, the Daoguang emperor (1820–1850) was still able to direct personally the huge and technically demanding job of rebuilding the whole Grand Canal artery. For the most part, however, one finds the central authority muddling along with too few personnel and too small a tax base for such a large empire. Along the coast and in the core parts of China proper, the late Qing approach became increasingly accommodationist, with ever wider grants of authority given to merchant guilds (such as the famous *cohong*, which from 1760 had charge of all foreign trade in Canton). Judicial, educational, social welfare, and a range of other functions were more and more conceded to local lineages, self-organized along Confucian lines.

The Qing government's approach was otherwise along the frontiers, heavily populated by non-Chinese ethnic groups or by Chinese-speaking Muslims (Hui). Here, the late Qing regime preferred violent repression to negotiation and accommodation. There was a special difficulty with Qing rule over Muslims in Yunnan and Xinjiang, both Hui as well as Turkic-speaking Muslims, the people later known as Uighurs (not directly related to the Uighur Turks prominent in Tang times). Acquired for mainly strategic reasons by Qianlong, Xinjiang was for many decades an albatross, requiring economic and financial assistance from China proper. And whereas the Qing emperors could convincingly assert leadership over Confucians, Chinese and Tibetan Buddhists, Catholic Christians, Manchus, Mongols, Tibetans, and Chinese, they could never pose as spiritual leaders of Muslims. They had to rule Muslims indirectly, through local *begs* and *khwājas*. In Yunnan, Qing forces and ethnic Chinese militias cooperated in massacres of the Hui, which eventually provoked the bloody Panthay rebellion of 1856–1873. In Xinjiang, beginning in the 1820s, Han Chinese officials pushed a powerful new agenda of encouraging massive Han (ethnic Chinese) immigration so as to transform the region and bring it fully within the orbit of Chinese civilization. That was not accomplished without challenge. A series of *jihād*-style attacks on Xinjiang from the Muslim Khoqand khanate west of the Pamirs led in 1832 to an "unequal treaty," whereby the Qing ceded to Khoqand commercial and other rights in western Xinjiang. (This action bore some resemblance to the extraterritorial concessions the Qing made to Britain in 1842, after the Opium War). Violence in and over Xinjiang continued for another half century—and, indeed, up to the present day.

In 1850 there lay in China's immediate future internal rebellions of historically unprecedented scale (especially the Taiping and Nian rebellions of 1850–1868). Regional authorities, using traditional methods, eventually suppressed these, even while China was under historically unprecedented pressure from the newly industrialized West. The Opium War of 1839–1842 was just the first in a series of wars and demands designed to force the Qing to open its ports and its markets to foreign commerce and to compel the empire to deal with the West in accordance with Western legal and diplomatic norms. During the first half of the twentieth century, the old system collapsed completely. The dynastic state was trashed. Revolutionary elites targeted the old-style extended Confucian family for destruction. Confucian doctrines were utterly discredited. But now, in the early part of the twenty-first century, there has been taking place from the bottom a surprising recrudescence of parts of the traditional institutional repertoire, including a revival of the extended family system and of the teaching of Confucian ethics. It remains to be seen whether a hereditary leadership (as in North Korea) will eventually emerge or, much more likely, a continuation of something vaguely like the old examination-based meritocracy, a new mandarinate of degree-holders in engineering and business management that would hold the dominant role in the governance of the country.

Social Institutions in Political Context

The question of the ways in which the people of China engaged with the state, or withdrew from it, or rebelled against it, is exceedingly complex. The further back in time one probes, the harder it becomes to fix a confident social perspective on it. Generally speaking, the earlier the time period, the more surviving sources consist of centrally focused histories and other compendia, and often only archaeology can help provide a window into life at ground level. By the Ming and especially the Qing, however, the rise of population, the spread of literacy, and the growth of book printing and publishing created such an overwhelming mass of local and family records, much of which still survives, that no one person can ever hope to read it all. But early or late, the imperial state, which at times seemed to exist only for its own sake, had to help shape, or at least accommodate itself to, the broad institutional contours of the people that it ruled. It was probably the early Ming state that went the furthest of all in its forceful attempt to remake Chinese society institutionally.

When one looks at the whole period from 150 to 1850, a trend that stands out is the rise to prominence and then the slow decline of religious institutions. Through early Tang times, Buddhist temples and temple estates in the countryside acted as little central points for economic redevelopment and as schools and welfare agencies for the people nearby. Then from at least the ninth century, and extending well into the Song and beyond, the Buddhist and Daoist churches, with their physical infrastructure, their sizable communities of monks and nuns, their state patronage, their holy sites small and large, and the private fervor and devotion they attracted, underwent a long process of decline. Yet they never disappeared altogether. There were occasional revivals, such as the late Ming Buddhist revival. Both Buddhist and Daoist temples certainly remained part of the urban landscape, even as their physical presence in the countryside shrank, often by forcible dispossession, their place taken by Confucian schools and corporate lineage estates.

Until Ming times, roughly speaking, the Buddhist establishment had been able to ingratiate itself with China's age-old preoccupations with ancestors, tomb rituals, family, and filial piety. But the leaders of the Neo-Confucian movement of Song times and later laid the intellectual groundwork for what turned out to be the successful rescue of China's familial institutions from the embrace of the churches. This involved the development of rules and formats for the composition of genealogies; the development of authoritative guidebooks for the conduct of family rituals (coming of age, marriage, death, and posthumous worship); the creation of regulations for the rearing and education of children; and rules for the carrying out of daily family governance.

Until the Yuan period, there was a limitation, reemphasized by no less an authority than Zhu Xi, on how far a family could legitimately expand the size and scale of its formal organization. The Confucian classics (and Tang "aristocratic" precedent) placed limits on the number of generations back in time a family could reach in identifying and worshipping an "original" ancestor. Peasants could go no further back than a grandfather. Educated men could go further back, how far depending upon how high they had risen in state service. Of course, the further back one was allowed to go to identify an ancestor, the larger the group of descendants presently living that could be gathered together as a coherent lineage. The only way for peasants or merchants legitimately to circumvent that severe size restriction was somehow to found a family all of whose male descendants agreed not to divide their inheritance, but to keep living together communally on an undivided estate (thus the famous Zheng family, commoners of Pujiang county in Zhejiang; and the Lu family, drug merchants in Jinxi in Jiangxi, kinsmen of Zhu Xi's philosophical rival, Lu Xiangshan). But these were fairly rare occurrences.

In the Yuan, curiously, it was a Mongol law relating to widows—together with a Neo-Confucian desideratum—that broke these longstanding limitations on family-based organization in China and opened the way to the formation of the large lineages that became, not rarities, but quite typical features of Chinese society in the Ming and Qing. Mongol law compelled the widow to remain in the family of her dead husband, where her labor and assets remained at her husband's family's disposal. She herself could be forced to marry one of her husband's relatives. Applied to China, the law was soon adjusted along Confucian lines to allow the widow not to remarry a relative of her dead husband's if she so chose; but in 1330, the Ministry of Rites further ordained that if a wife or widow left her husband's family, she had to leave her assets behind, and that only her dead husband's family could arrange a remarriage for her. This put an end to the Song rule that gave women personal control of their dowries and other assets and, if widowed, permitted them to return to their natal families and remarry whomever they chose. This ruling had a direct impact on litigation in the courts of the county magistrates and so led by degrees to the creation of stronger lineages nationwide. By 1350, in parts of south China (especially southern Anhui), one could find local elites writing and updating lineage genealogies, building Confucian-style ancestral temples, and funding ritual gatherings and elementary schooling from the proceeds of endowed corporate estates. (In 1000 CE, hardly any of that would have existed. Northern Song society, in its intense focus on the central state, was more closely comparable to early Tang society than to the much more heavily localized Ming or Qing.)

The spread was gradual. Only from the mid-Ming (the sixteenth century) did lineages fully form in Fujian, Guangdong, Jiangxi, the lower Yangzi region, Shaanxi, and elsewhere. First came arduous research efforts. Often it was the aspiring lineage's junior literati who volunteered, or were asked, to locate and identify all knowable ancestors, account for descendants, compile and publish the results, and persuade senior officials who were also well-known literati (but usually not members of the lineage itself) to validate the completed genealogy by writing an approving preface for it.

That was early on. After a couple of generations, there emerged among the high literati a willingness to overlook problems of poor or missing evidence that had inhibited the earlier genealogists and to agree to endorse the construction of large associations of kinsmen sharing the same surname whose exact genealogical relationships were often murky. Individual landowners were persuaded to donate land or money to the building of main and branch ancestral temples, whose endowments might be used to fund any or all of a range of purposes: periodic rituals; schooling for children and juniors; food relief and other assistance to the poor; help in emigrating to other parts of China; land reclamation; business investments; litigation on behalf of members; local antibandit defense; and so on. The extent and scale of lineage formation, and the purposes to which lineage corporations were put, of course varied from one part of China to another—from the very highly organized and powerful lineages of Guangdong and Fujian to the smaller and often unendowed common-descent groups of north China, and all sorts of variants in between.

Aside from the change in the law that boosted patrilineal authority, there was another and quite different development that, inadvertently perhaps, helped local elites establish an identity and later form lineages. Following the horrific battering the rebellions and wars of the 1350s and 1360s inflicted upon China north and south, the early Ming dynasty, in its utopian drive to remake the civilization, intruded more deeply into society at ground level than any authority since the early Tang. This included the creation of a nationwide apparatus for the imposition of labor services in person and the collection of taxes in kind. County units were divided into cantons, cantons into townships, and, most important, townships into wards (*li*). Each ward, in theory, was made up of 110 landowning households, occupying a few square miles of land. The heads of the ten richest families shared management of the tax collections, for which they were personally liable in case of default. This was rural social organization as imposed from the early Ming center, at Nanjing. But this so-called *lijia* system, coercive as it may have been at the outset, soon established itself as a source of local social legitimacy: the descendants of the original leaders came to base their social status and honor, their very identity as local elites, upon their *lijia* membership as established early in Ming. This remained the case even after the labor-based *lijia* system itself yielded to the property-based "single whip" tax system during the sixteenth century.

Lijia institutionalized social status in another way. Taxes and services involved two forms of participation. People could provide physical labor, or they could provide supervision and management. The elite were, on the whole, willing to perform managerial duties, despite the risks. Uneducated men, smallholders or tenant farmers, did the actual hauling of the grain tax and performed required services such as policing, public works, running messages, and the like. The power to identify these workers, assign them their tasks, and direct their work fell to the heads of the richer landowning families. Thus, national policy contributed heavily to the solidification and perpetuation of a rather rigid rural class system across the length and breadth of China. The upper class of comparatively affluent and educated families typically gave themselves identifying choronyms, usually based upon the name of the ward they lived in (thus the "Peach Spring" Xiao lineage of Taihe county, Jiangxi, and many thousands more like it). By the sixteenth century, the enterprising individual landlords and estate builders of early Ming gave way to corporate boards of lineage managers. Informal organization yielded more and more to rule-bound procedures. As local economies came to be based heavily on silver, and as taxes in silver assessed upon land came to replace taxes in kind, the lineages developed corporate estates that could not easily be divided or sold and so escaped the leveling effects of China's system of partible family inheritance.

There was a dark side to the emerging lineage order. It was not poor people who were responsible for China's demographic growth (approximately a tripling during the Ming, and nearly again during the Qing); it was the educated and the affluent. They practiced polygyny and also female infanticide. Known population growth rates among the Ming upper (managerial) class show that it was capable of doubling its size about every seventy years. This should have led to a nationwide population approaching China's current population of 1.3 billion by the end of the Ming. Emigration from densely settled parts of China to new frontiers within China was what allowed the total Ming population to triple as it did. But the reason why population rose to nowhere near a billion was because the lineages regularly consigned some major portion of each new generation to downward social mobility. The scarcity of women created during each generation a large class of young men who could never hope to marry. Their usual fate was to become drifters, join gangs, turn to banditry, be sold, or sell themselves into bondage. Additionally, even in a province like Guangdong, heavily populated by powerful lineages, perhaps some 70 percent of the men of the province belonged to small or weak families that lacked special privileges or protection. Late imperial China came to feature a massive and unhappy reservoir of victims of debt, downward mobility, and bondage; a lower class of boatmen and porters, of drifters and bandits; of criminal gangs and sectarian adherents; of despised and legally disfranchised groups such as musicians, beggars, and the like that the Yongzheng emperor tried to emancipate in the 1720s and 1730s. There were more than sufficient labor reserves at hand to fuel the widespread bond servant rebellions and other disorders of the late Ming, as well as the huge Taiping and other upheavals that engulfed China in the middle of the nineteenth century.

The lineages of Ming and Qing times were extremely durable at the local level. They have been styled an "aristogeny." How did they differ from the so-called aristocracy of the age of disunion, Sui, and early Tang? For one, they were much more formally institutionalized. For another, their ties to central government, though still important, were much thinner. China's population growth over the preceding thousand years explains why: from fifty million or less to two or three hundred million and more, without a commensurate increase in the size of government. No lineage, or small group of lineages, could hereditarily dominate government in the Ming or Qing, as was sometimes possible in earlier times, especially given the hurdle of the open examination system and the constant personnel turnover it ensured.

China's social "great leap" from the restricted lineage group of earlier times to the open system of the Ming and Qing was mirrored, indeed anticipated, by the behavior of the imperial lineages of Song times and later. The Li imperial lineage of the Tang, which was managed by a special institution, the Court of the Imperial Clan, followed the classical models and reduced all distantly related kinsmen to commoner status. The Northern Song, ruled by the Zhao family of military origin, created a new pattern. Taking advantage of the ongoing debate in Confucian circles over the appropriate size of lineages, the Song court under Zhezong (r. 1086–1100) decided that the Zhao lineage should include all descendants and no longer observe the Tang-style restrictions. But also unlike the Tang, the Northern Song court from the outset barred all kinsmen from military or civil office and forced them to live in what has been called "functionless luxury" in the capital, Kaifeng. They were expensive to maintain; by the late eleventh century their numbers had swelled to some five thousand, and two satellite settlements had to be created for them elsewhere in north China. The Zhao kinsmen suffered grievously in the Jurchen invasion of the early twelfth century. The Southern Song made major changes in policy regarding the now much-reduced Zhao lineage. Members were afforded special access to the body of civil service examination candidates and, if successful in the competition, they were permitted to take office. Many did. Many more became military officers. Special lineage communities, funded by local resources, were placed in the wealthy Fujian port cities of Quanzhou and Fuzhou. By the end of the Southern Song, the imperial lineage had grown very large indeed, but it fell well short of the estimated eighty thousand males the Zhu lineage, descendants of Ming Taizu, reached by the early seventeenth century. Like their Northern Song counterparts, the Zhu were forbidden to take examinations or enter government by other means until as late as 1595. Despite enormous total annual allotments of grain, many distant Zhu relatives became poor. The imperial Aisin Gioro lineage of the Qing reached some twenty-nine thousand by the end of the dynasty. Members could take exams and had some access to power positions, unlike their Ming counterparts, and more in the style of the much smaller group of descendants of Chinggis Khan in Yuan China. The demographic behavior of the Ming emperors was very like that of the Chinese upper class generally—heavily lopsided sex ratios in favor of males; polygyny; and population growth rates approaching 2 percent per annum. All these imperial lineages seem to have been, on the whole, a useless drain, forced into parasitism and contributing little or nothing to the economy, the security, or the political leadership of the country.

Lineages—these private, kin-based corporations based in Confucian doctrine—did not exist in defiance of the imperial state. Indeed, they owed their existence to the state's protective embrace. Lineage leadership, almost without exception, consisted of men who had secured honors, exemptions, titles, offices of many kinds, and academic degrees from the imperial state. The rarest plum in the recognition-granting cornucopia that the state controlled was of course the metropolitan examination degree (*jinshi*), earned in an intense series of competition rounds and almost a guarantee of high office, fame, and wealth. And there were countless other, less distinguished tokens that the state might confer. Each such token guaranteed the recipient a certain level of privileged relationship to the world of government. Since Tang times, the examination system produced many more educated aspirants than could ever hope to obtain actual bureaucratic positions. It was this great surplus that made possible the strongly localist turns that China took in the Southern Song, the Yuan, and again in the mid-Ming and the early Qing. The central state's reaction to these localist turns was to offer friendly support, but also to train a suspicious and wary eye on them. Lineages were not incorruptible. Their leaders were always tempted to disown the poor and the weak, sell genealogical credentials to rich interlopers, and fight other lineages over such desirable resources as tomb sites, fields, markets, and water rights. Like little empires, lineages were also prone to keep expanding in size and power until forcibly stopped. Yet, it was by recruiting Hunan lineages that Zeng Guofan was able to create forces large and powerful enough to suppress the Taiping rebellion in the 1860s. Clearly, the existence of lineages was more an advantage than a disadvantage to the late imperial state system.

The civil service examination system of the Ming and Qing was a colossal national enterprise conducted according to a rigid schedule with utterly dependable regularity. For the most part it was diligently policed, so major fraud, corruption, and scandal were rather rare.

It may be useful to an understanding of the system to follow the career of a hypothetical child and later adult as he negotiated all the rungs of the ladder. Perhaps the child's immediate family was poor, but the elders of the larger lineage of which his family was a component noticed the boy's academic talent and so invited him to join his young cousins in the lineage elementary school. This prepared him for his first hurdle, a test to qualify as a licentiate, a local government student, when he reached the approximate age of sixteen. There were in all some 1,500 prefectures and counties with government schools, with paid instructors who early in the Ming actually taught the students; but the schools soon evolved into registration and testing centers only, leaving the students to seek instruction in private Confucian academies or in their own informal study circles. The status of these licentiates was probationary—they had to keep requalifying by frequent testing. At the beginning of the Ming, all licentiates (twenty in each county, forty in each prefecture) received stipends. During the course of the fifteenth century, the student body quota was repeatedly expanded, eventually to permit the registration of all qualified aspirants, but without stipends. Nationwide, the local student body grew from some fifty thousand in 1500 to some five hundred thousand in 1700. The licentiates often led culturally and intellectually rich lives in their home localities. The Ming and Qing capital cities (Nanjing, then Beijing) exerted much less attraction than Chang'an in early Tang or Kaifeng in the Northern Song. And by the late Ming, lowly licentiate status was no longer a bar to literary fame: Chen Jiru (1558–1639), Pu Songling (1640–1715), and Wu Jingzi (1701–1754) are but three outstanding examples. The vast majority of licentiates, however, had to turn to humbler sources of income, such as teaching, estate management, tax engrossment, or litigation.

The goal of every licentiate was to clear the next hurdle, the award of a provincial degree. Every three years, several thousand licentiates were certified to gather in their provincial capital for a competitive test that took three days and two nights. Here, a strict quota of around a hundred passers ensured a failure rate of about 95 percent. Licentiates might try these exams many times. The chance was extremely small that any one licentiate would ever achieve the degree, but winning it meant a great deal: permanent elite status, eligibility for official position, and important tax and legal exemptions.

That was not the top of the ladder. In the year following each provincial examination, all of those who had passed gathered in Beijing for the metropolitan round. At this level the failure rate was still upwards of 90 percent, with some four thousand provincial degree-winners competing for three hundred available metropolitan degrees. (The competition was not totally meritocratic; in order to ensure national integration, the quota system was configured in such a way as to provide opportunities for less well-prepared candidates from the north China and border provinces, which lagged behind the south economically and culturally.) Nor was this the top. There immediately followed a palace examination nominally conducted by the emperor himself, according to the results of which a final ranking of 1 to 300 was established. The top finishers were taken into that great literary think tank, the Hanlin Academy, a training ground for later appointment to the best positions in the central bureaucracy. Those toward the bottom of the list typically were sent out to the counties of the realm to begin their careers as local magistrates. (The appointments system placed these men anywhere but in their native provinces and usually put new men in small and quiet counties, not in busy and difficult ones.) The average age of metropolitan degree-winners was about thirty-one.

However, it is a fact that the majority of the positions in this rather exclusive mandarinate consisted of very low posts such as vice and assistant magistrates, fishery monopoly directors, instructors in the government school system, and the like; typically it was not provincial or metropolitan degree-holders who filled these posts, but rather men promoted up from the clerical service, or degree-seeking licentiates who repeatedly failed, were then sent to (or purchased status in) the national Confucian college, and, after a very long wait, were finally offered appointments. These men were at times forbidden promotion to the elite ranks. Bureaucracy thus featured a kind of internal caste system as an outgrowth of its meritocratic principles.

The higher officials of the Ming and Qing bureaucracy usually had no direct contact with the public but spent much of their time studying, supervising, criticizing, and periodically rating the work of other officials lower in the hierarchy. It was county magistrates, and officials below that rank, who regularly met the public in connection with such functions as tax assessment and collection, disaster relief, bandit suppression, litigation, and education. The system was laced with fines and other penalties for administrative misdemeanors and mistakes, so much so that by the middle of the eighteenth century office holding tended to become such an unpleasant experience as to prompt early resignations and truncated careers. After the completion of Qing empire building in the 1760s, it tended more and more to be the case that high-ranking civil officials, Chinese graduates of the examination system, were given the personally risky and less-than-glamorous tasks of organizing and commanding the military suppression of rebellions (such as the White Lotus rebellion of 1796–1805) and troubles along the frontiers in the southwest, and in Sichuan, Xinjiang, and Tibet.

Much of history entails paradox. Certainly, late imperial China is a case in point, an overstretched Manchu-run regime, with too small a government, army, and tax base for its huge territory and society, strong enough to do impressive things and survive extraordinary shocks yet also observably shaky and vulnerable even in the best of times. Some European visitors noted this. In the 1550s, Galeote Pereira thought Ming China conquerable by a good European army. European onlookers were puzzled as to how a small and culturally primitive folk like the Manchus were able to seize control of so large and sophisticated a place as late Ming China. In the early 1700s, when the Kangxi emperor was still ruling, John Bell thought China could be conquered by Russia. In the 1740s, English sea captain Anson was struck by China's palpable military weakness. Macartney, leader of the famous but failed 1793 British embassy to China, made several remarkable comments about the institutional complexion of the Qing empire. He marveled that, unlike the case of the Hanoverian dynasty that ruled Britain and became British, the few Manchus that ruled three hundred million Chinese, from the Qianlong emperor on down to the lowliest soldiers, managed to preserve an ethnic distinctiveness. He was amazed that a dynasty and a government, unloved by the people it ruled, could yet perform such an intricate and demanding task as to keep the huge realm under some semblance of oversight and control. But, he stated, "I often perceived the ground to be hollow under a vast superstructure."[1] He thought the empire might well collapse in his own lifetime. "Frequent insurrections in distant provinces"[2] were clear warning signs of that. Macartney was wrong only by a century. He died in 1806. The Qing ended in 1912.

---

1. J. L. Cranmer-Byng, ed. *An Embassy to China: Being the Journal Kept by Lord Macartney during His Embassy to the Emperor Ch'ien-lung 1793–1794* (London: Longmans, Green and Co. Ltd., 1962), 239.
2. Ibid., 238.

Further Reading

A proper bibliography of books, articles, and chapter-length studies in English would turn out to be impossibly long, and longer by a factor of three or four if one were to include all the work available in modern Chinese, Japanese, and the principal languages of Europe. As a search of the Internet will turn up several book lists, maps, and timelines prepared by teachers of Chinese history, let me just comment here on a limited number of contributions, some old but most new, that have struck me as interesting, well written, not too specialized or theorized, and reliably grounded in the original sources. Inevitably I will sin by omission, and I must apologize to the many authors to whose work I am indebted but cannot begin to list here.

For the whole period from 150 to 1850, the multivolume *Cambridge History of China*, originally edited by Denis Twitchett and John K. Fairbank, is slowly nearing completion, and contains many very readable chapters on dynasties, rulers, and events. F. W. Mote's *Imperial China, 900–1800* (Cambridge: Harvard University Press, 1999) is, despite its great bulk of over a thousand pages, a comprehensive account that keeps the general reader in mind. Interesting and thought provoking is S. A. M. Adshead's *China in World History* (3rd ed., New York: St. Martin's Press, 2000). Almost forty years after publication, the same can still be said of Mark Elvin, *The Pattern of the Chinese Past* (Stanford: Stanford University Press, 1973). Charles Horner attempts to link present-day China back into its Yuan, Ming, and Qing past in his interesting *Rising China and Its Postmodern Fate: Memories of Empire in a New Global Context* (Athens: University of Georgia Press, 2009). Unexpectedly readable is Endymion Wilkinson, *Chinese History: A Manual, Revised and Enlarged* (Harvard University Press, 2000).

Most of the available publications dealing with the years from 150 to 589, an age of flux and disunion, focus either on religion or on literature. However, Albert E. Dien's *Six Dynasties Civilization* (New Haven: Yale University Press, 2007) gives prominence to archeology and material culture. The work of Arthur F. Wright, especially

Buddhism in Chinese History (Stanford University Press, 1959), and *The Sui Dynasty* (New York: Alfred A. Knopf, 1978), is first rate. W. J. F. Jenner's *Memories of Loyang: Yang Hsüan-chih and the Lost Capital, 493–534* (Oxford: Clarendon Press, 1981) provides excellent perspective and detail on north China in the turbulent fourth through sixth centuries.

No survey of the Tang can fail to mention the absorbing works of Edward H. Schafer: *The Golden Peaches of Samarkand: A Study of T'ang Exotics* (Berkeley: University of California Press, 1963), and *The Vermilion Bird: T'ang Images of the South* (University of California Press, 1967). David A. Graff's *Medieval Chinese Warfare, 200–900* (London and New York: Routledge, 2002) presents its subject with clarity. Tang history finds itself effectively intertwined with biography in the lives of some leading literary figures, for instance in James J. Y. Liu, *The Poetry of Li Shang-yin: A Ninth-Century Baroque Chinese Poet* (Chicago: University of Chicago Press, 1969); Charles Hartman, *Han Yü and the T'ang Search for Unity* (Princeton: Princeton University Press, 1986); and Robin D. S. Yates, *Washing Silk: The Life and Selected Poetry of Wei Chuang, 834?–910* (Harvard University Press, 1988).

Despite a growing body of scholarship on the Liao, Song, Jin, and Xi Xia, most books about this era are specialized, and few pass the stern tests of significance and readability. James T. C. Liu's *China Turning Inward: Intellectual-Political Changes in the Twelfth Century* (Harvard University Press, 1988) comes close. There is also Ronald C. Egan, *Word, Image, and Deed in the Life of Su Shi* (Harvard University Press, 1994).

The leading work on the Mongols in China is Morris Rossabi, *Khubilai Khan: His Life and Times* (University of California Press, 1988). The underwater archaeology of Khubilai's failed naval attacks on Japan has been well described by James P. Delgado, *Khubilai Khan's Lost Fleet: In Search of a Legendary Armada* (University of California Press, 2003). Recently, Stephen G. Haw has intelligently addressed a never-ending interest in his *Marco Polo's China: A Venetian in the Realm of Khubilai Khan* (Routledge, 2006).

Several good books help illuminate the long history of Ming China. Sarah Schneewind, *A Tale of Two Melons: Emperor and Subject in Ming China* (Indianapolis and Cambridge: Hackett Publishing

Company, 2006) deals with the slipperiness of such intimate interchanges as took place been the ruling center and people in the localities of the early Ming. The Ming naval voyages to Southeast Asia and Africa have been elegantly discussed in Louise Levathes, *When China Ruled the Seas: The Treasure Fleet of the Dragon Throne, 1405–1433* (New York and Oxford: Oxford University Press, 1994). Also readable, and better from a technical viewpoint, is Edward L. Dreyer, *Zheng He: China and the Oceans in the Early Ming Dynasty* (New York: Pearson Longman, 2006). Well written and still interesting is Ray Huang, *1587: A Year of No Significance—The Ming Dynasty in Decline* (Yale University Press, 1981). Not to be missed is Arthur Waldron, *The Great Wall of China: From History to Myth* (New York: Cambridge University Press, 1990).

The seventeenth century and the Ming-Qing transition have been extensively written about, thanks to copious sources, the presence in China of Europeans, mainly Jesuits, and a deepening global dimension to economic and other history. Frederick Wakeman Jr., *The Great Enterprise: The Manchu Reconstruction of Order in Seventeenth-Century China* (2 vols., University of California Press, 1985) looks forbidding but is illustrated and quite readable. Lynn A. Struve, *The Southern Ming: 1644–1662* (Yale University Press, 1984) is a vivid narrative of its subject. There are several good books on the Jesuits in China; most recent and interesting is Liam Matthew Brockey, *Journey to the East: The Jesuit Mission to China, 1579–1724* (Harvard University Press, 2007). Jonathan D. Spence is the talented author or editor of no fewer than six works on this era, including *The Death of Woman Wang* (New York: Viking Press, 1978), featuring local governance in a poverty-stricken part of seventeenth-century north China, and *Emperor of China: A Self-Portrait of K'ang-hsi* (Alfred A. Knopf, 1974).

The high Qing—meaning, for the most part, the Qianlong reign, 1735–1799—has been illuminated by some exceptionally interesting offerings. Let me simply list some in chronological order of their publication: Harold L. Kahn, *Monarchy in the Emperor's Eyes: Image and Reality in the Ch'ien-lung Reign* (Harvard University Press, 1971); Philip A. Kuhn, *Soulstealers: The Chinese Sorcery Scare of 1768* (Harvard University Press, 1990); Alain Peyrefitte, *The Immobile Empire* (Alfred A. Knopf, 1992); James A. Millward, *Beyond the Pass:*

Economy, Ethnicity, and Empire in Qing Central Asia, 1759–1864 (Stanford University Press, 1998); Jonathan D. Spence, *Treason by the Book* (Viking, 2001); and Peter C. Perdue, *China Marches West: The Qing Conquest of Central Eurasia* (Harvard University Press, 2005).

The Opium War of 1839–1842 has traditionally been taken to be the starting point for the history of modern China, and the many good books on the topic will not be covered here. Although the earlier years of the nineteenth century have not been intensively investigated, there does exist one superb study: Jane Kate Leonard, *Controlling from Afar: The Daoguang Emperor's Management of the Grand Canal Crisis, 1824–1826* (Ann Arbor: Center for Chinese Studies, University of Michigan, 1996).

INDEX

Aguda, 44
Aizong (Jurchen Jin ruler), 49
Altan Khan, 76, 77
An Lushan rebellion, 21, 27, 28, 32, 47, 60
Annam, 33, 43; see also Vietnam
Arughtai, 70–71

Beijing, 49, 50, 52, 57, 70, 72, 82
Bianzhou, 33; see also Kaifeng
Buddhism/Buddhist church, 9, 11, 13, 15, 22, 25, 31, 45, 61, 70, 92
bureaucratic recruitment, xiv–xv, 20–21, 53, 64, 99–101

Cai Jing, 43
Cao Cao, 4, 6, 14
Cao Pi, 5, 6
Chan Buddhism, 31
Chang'an, 19, 22, 25, 26, 27, 28, 30, 32, 33
Chen dynasty, 16, 18
Chen Jiru, 99
Cheng (Cheng-Han) dynasty, 7
Cheng Yi, 43
Chongzhen (Ming ruler), 80
Chouchi, 10
Confucianism, xvii, 30–31, 45, 48; see also Neo-Confucianism
Cui Hao, 13

Dai (regime), 12
Dalai lamas, 80, 83, 87
Dali, 42, 62
Daoguang (Qing ruler), 90
Daoist church, 13, 22, 25, 49, 61, 92
daoxue, see Neo-Confucianism

Dezong (Tang ruler), 29
Di (tribe), 6, 9, 10, 11, 12, 13, 17
Donglin, 73, 79
Dorgon, 82
Du Guangting, 33
Dutch, 77, 78, 85

Eastern Jin dynasty, 9, 15–16, 85
Eight Princes, War of the, 7–8
Erzhu Rong, 15, 17
Esen, 72
eunuchs, 3, 30, 33, 56–57, 72, 79
examination system, see bureaucratic recruitment

Fan Wencheng, 61
Fang Guozhen, 55
Fang La, 44
Fang Xiaoru, 69
Fei River battle, 12
Feng (Northern Wei empress), 13
Five Dynasties and Ten Kingdoms, 33–35, 38–39
Former Liang dynasty, 7
Former Qin dynasty, 11
Former Yan dynasty, 7, 10
Former Zhao dynasty, 9
Fotudeng, 9, 13
Fu Jian (Former Qin ruler), 10, 12, 16, 25

Galdan, 87
Gao Huan, 16, 17
Gao Jiong, 22
Gao Yang, 17
Gaozong (Tang ruler), 26
Gaozong (Southern Song ruler), 45, 46

Geng Jingzhong, 84
Gongsun warlords, 4
Grand Canal, 22, 25, 29, 64, 65, 66, 70, 90
Grand Council, 89
Great Rites Controversy, 74
Great Shu dynasty, 34–35
Great Wall, 71
Gu Yanwu, 59

Han dynasty, see Later Han dynasty
Han Yu, 30
Hešen, 89
Hong Chengchou, 80, 83
Hongxi (Ming ruler), 71–72
Hou Jing, 17
Hu (Northern Wei empress), 15
Huan Wen, 16
Huang Chao rebellion, 32–33
Huang Zongxi, 59
Hui (Chinese Muslims), 90–91
Huizong (Northern Song ruler), 43, 44
Hung Taiji (Qing ruler), 80

Japan/Japanese, 75, 76, 79, 85
Jesuits, 78, 84, 87, 88
Jia Sidao, 50
Jiajing (Ming ruler), 72, 73–76
Jianwen (Ming ruler), 69
Jie (tribe), 9, 10, 15, 17
Jin (Jurchen) dynasty, 36, 44, 45–47, 48, 49, 61, 64
Jingtai (Ming ruler), 72

Kaifeng, 40, 41, 44, 46, 49, 81
Kangxi (Qing ruler), 83, 84–88
Khitans, 47, 64; see also Liao dynasty
Khubilai (Yuan ruler), 60, 61–63
Koguryŏ, 23, 27

Kou Qianzhi, 13
Koxinga, see Zheng Chenggong
Kumarajiva, 12

Later Han dynasty, 3–4, 5, 29
Later Jin dynasty, 40
Later Liang dynasty (386–403), 12
Later Liang dynasty (sixth century), 17
Later Liang dynasty (tenth century), 67
Later Qin dynasty, 12
Later Tang dynasty, 40
Later Yan dynasty, 12
Later Zhao dynasty, 9
Later Zhou dynasty, 40
Li Ao, 30
Li Gang, 44
Li Jiqian, 40
Li Keyong, 33
Li Linfu, 28
Li Shimin (Tang ruler), 24, 26, 69
Li Te (Cheng ruler), 7
Li Yuan (Tang ruler), 23, 27
Li Zicheng, 80–81
Liao dynasty, 36, 37, 39–40, 43, 44, 49
lijia system, 95
lineages, Ming and Qing, 96–97
Liu Bei, 5
Liu Cong, 8, 9
Liu Ji, xvii, 67
Liu Yao, 9
Liu Yu, 16
Liu Zongyuan, 30
Lizong (Southern Song ruler), 50
Lu Xiangshan, 93
Lu Zhi, 29
Lü Guang, 12
Lü Kun, xviii
Luoyang, 4, 7, 9, 14, 15, 22, 26, 28, 32, 42, 50

Macartney, Lord, 101–102
Manchus, 58–61, 83
Meng Zhixiang, 35
Ming dynasty, xviii, 66–82
Ming Taizu, *see* Zhu Yuanzhang
Murong (Xianbi clan), 6, 7, 9, 10, 12

Nanzhao, 28, 29, 31, 32, 33
Neiwufu, 57–58
New Policies, 42, 43, 48
Neo-Confucianism (*daoxue*), xvii, 42, 48, 50, 53, 60, 64, 70, 73
Nerchinsk treaty, 84, 87
non-Chinese rule, xvii–xviii, 1–2
Northern Qi dynasty, 17
Northern Song dynasty, 35, 37, 38, 40–45, 47
Northern Wei dynasty, 12–15, 19, 24
Northern Yan dynasty, 13
Northern Zhou dynasty, 17, 18, 19
Nurhaci, 79

Oyirads, 70–71, 72

Pan Jixun, 77
Pang Xun, 32
Parhae, 33
Peach Blossom Spring, 1
Pingcheng, 12, 14
Portuguese, 75, 76, 78, 79, 85
Pu Songling, 99

Qi Biaojia, xviii
Qi Jiguang, 76, 77
Qian Liu, 33, 34
Qiang (tribe), 6, 9, 12, 13, 17, 36
Qianlong (Qing ruler), 88, 89–91
Qiao Zhou, 5
Qing dynasty, 82–91

Qinzong (Northern Song ruler), 44

Ran Min, 10
Red Cliffs battle, 5
Red Turban rebellion, xvi, 65–66, 67
Restoration Society, 80
Ricci, Matteo, 78
Russia, 87

semu, 63–64
Shang Kexi, 84
shanyu, 27
Shanyuan treaty, 41
Shatuo (tribe), 32, 33, 39
Shence Army, 30, 32
Shenzong (Northern Song ruler), 42, 43
Shi Hu, 10
Shi Jingtang, 39
Shi Lang, 86
Shi Le, 8, 9, 10, 13, 25
Shizong (Jurchen Jin ruler), 47
Shu-Han dynasty, 5
Shun dynasty, 81–82
Shunzhi (Qing ruler), 82–83
Silla, 33
Sima family, 6–8
Sima Guang, 43
Six Garrisons, Revolt of the, 15, 27
Song dynasty, 21; *see also* Northern Song dynasty, Southern Song dynasty
Song Lian, 67
Song Taizu, *see* Zhao Kuangyin
Southern Han dynasty, 34
Southern Liang dynasty, 16, 17
Southern Ming (era), 84–86
Southern Song dynasty, 45–51, 85
Southern Tang dynasty, 34, 35

Spanish, 77, 78, 85
Su Chuo, 18, 42
Su Shi, 43
Su Wei, 22
Sui dynasty, 18, 19–23
Sun Quan, 5
Suzong (Tang ruler), 28

Taichang (Ming ruler), 79
Taihe Reforms, 14
Taiwu (Northern Wei ruler), 13
Taizong (Tang ruler), see Li Shimin
Tang dynasty, 20–21, 24–34
Tangut (tribe, language), 36, 46, 63
Tao Qian, 1
Three Kingdoms (era), 5–6
Tianqi (Ming ruler), 79–80
Tibet, 28, 31, 33, 45, 70, 87
Toghto, 65–66
Tong Guan, 43, 44
Tujue (tribe), 23, 25, 27, 28
Tuoba (Xianbi clan), 6, 9, 12, 15
Tuyuhun (tribe), 6, 27, 32

Uighurs, 28, 29, 31–32, 33, 36, 40, 90

Vietnam, 71; see also Annam

Wang Anshi, 42, 47
Wang Chonggu, 77
Wang Jian, 33, 34
Wang Yangming, 73, 75
Wanli (Ming ruler), 79
Wanyan Liang, 46
Wei (Cao-Wei) dynasty, 5–6
Wei Zhuang, 33
Wei Zhongxian, 79–80
Wen Tianxiang, 51, 58, 85
Wendi (Sui ruler), see Yang Jian
Western Jin dynasty, 1, 6–8, 19

Western Wei dynasty, 17
Western Yan dynasty, 12
Wu dynasty, 5, 7
Wu (Northern Zhou ruler), 18, 26
Wu (Tang empress), 24, 26
Wu Jingzi, 99
Wu Sangui, 82, 84
Wu-Yue, 34
Wudi (Southern Liang ruler), 25
Wuzong (Tang ruler), 31

Xi Xia dynasty, 36, 37, 40, 41, 43, 45, 49, 62
xian (county), xiii
Xia Yan, 75–76
Xianbi (tribe), 12, 13, 14, 17, 26
Xianzong (Tang ruler), 30
Xiao Cha, 17
Xiao (Uighur clan), 39
Xiaowen (Northern Wei ruler), 14
Xie An, 16
Xiongnu (tribe), 6, 8, 13
Xizong (Tang ruler), 33
Xu Heng, 60
Xuande (Ming ruler), 72
Xuanzang, 25
Xuanzong (Tang ruler), 26, 28
Xuanzong (Jurchen Jin ruler), 47

Yan Song, 76
Yang Jian (Sui ruler), 18, 19, 22, 23
Yang Tinghe, 74
Yangdi (Sui ruler), 23, 26
Yao Chang (Later Qin ruler), 12
Yellow Turban rebellion, ix, xiv, xx, 4, 65
Yelü Abaoji (Liao ruler), 39
Yelü Bei, 39
Yongle (Ming ruler), 69–71
Yongzheng (Qing ruler), 88
Yu Qian, 72
Yuan dynasty, 61–66

Yue Fei, 46
Yuwen (Xianbi clan), 6, 9, 18
Yuwen Hu, 18
Yuwen Tai, 17
Yuwen Rong, 27

Zhang Bin, 9
Zhang Dai, xviii
Zhang Daoling, 4
Zhang Gui (Former Liang ruler), 7
Zhang Juzheng, 73, 76–77, 79
Zhang Xianzhong, 80–81
Zhangzong (Jurchen Jin ruler), 47
Zhao Ding, 46
Zhao Kuangyin (Northern Song ruler), 40
Zheng He, 70
Zheng Chenggong, 85–86
Zhengtong (Ming ruler), 72
Zhezong (Northern Song ruler), 43, 97
Zhu Di, *see* Yongle
Zhu Wen, 33, 34
Zhu Xi, 48, 50, 53, 64, 73, 74–75, 93
Zhu Yuanzhang (Ming ruler), 54–56, 58–59, 66–69
Zhuge Liang, 5
Zunghars, 87, 88, 89